AF662126

Human, Economic and Environmental Geography

Human, Economic and Environmental Geography

Professor Meenu Agrawal
Principal and Head, Department of Economics,
Ginni Devi Modi Girls (Post-graduate) College, Modinagar

New Century Publications
New Delhi, India

New Century Publications
4800 / 24, Bharat Ram Road,
Ansari Road, Daryaganj,
New Delhi - 110 002 (India)

Tel.: 011-2324 7798, 4358 7398, 4101 7798
E-mail: info@newcenturypublications.com
www.newcenturypublications.com

Editorial office:
LG – 7, Aakarshan Bhawan,
4754-57/23, Ansari Road, Daryaganj,
New Delhi – 110 002

Tel.: 011-4356 0919

Copyright © 2019 by the author

All rights reserved. No part of this book may be reproduced, stored in a retrieval system, or transmitted in any form or by any means, mechanical, photocopying, recording, or otherwise without the prior written permission of the publisher.

First Published: **2019**

ISBN: **978-81-7708-488-7**

Published by New Century Publications and printed at Milan Enterprises, New Delhi.

Designs: Patch Creative Unit, New Delhi.

PRINTED IN INDIA

About the Book

Human geography is a branch of geography that deals with the study of people and their communities, cultures, economies, and interactions with the environment by studying their relations with and across space and place. Human geography attends to human patterns of social interaction, as well as spatial level interdependencies, and how they influence or affect Earth's environment. It concentrates on the study of human activities by using qualitative and quantitative research methods.

Economic geography is the study of place, distribution and spatial organization of economic activities across the world. It represents a traditional sub field of the discipline of geography. However, many economists have also approached it in ways more typical of the discipline of economics.

Economic geography is also defined by the geographers as the study of human economic activities under varying sets of conditions associated with production, location, distribution, consumption, and exchange of resources.

Environmental geography is a branch of geography that describes the spatial aspects of interactions between humans and the natural world. It is the study of systematic description of different components of environment and interaction of human beings with these components.

This book explains and examines various facets of the three related subjects of human, economic and environmental geography.

About the Author

Professor Meenu Agrawal is Principal, Ginni Devi Modi Girls (Post-graduate) College, Modinagar, Uttar Pradesh and also Associate Professor and Head, Department of Economics in the same college. She obtained her Ph.D. degree from Ch. Charan Singh University, Meerut in 1991. She specialises in the areas of rural development, economic choices and environmental issues. With more than 35 years of teaching experience and 25 years of research experience, she has authored 42 books and co-authored 17 books in areas of her specialisation.

Dr. Agrawal has published 75 research papers in journals and magazines of repute. She has also attended and presented papers at various national and international conferences and seminars. She has also organized 10 national seminars, sponsored by the University Grants Commission (UGC), New Delhi and the Indian Council of Social Science Research (ICSSR), New Delhi. She is the recipient of several awards at the national level.

Contents

Part II: Economic Geography

Part III: Environmental Geography

Preface

Geography as a discipline is divided into the sub-fields of physical geography and human geography, the latter concentrating upon the study of human activities by the application of qualitative and quantitative research methods. Human geography is the branch of geography that deals with the study of people and their communities, cultures, economies, and interactions with the environment by studying their relations with and across space and place. Human geography attends to human patterns of social interaction, as well as spatial level inter-dependencies, and how they influence or affect the earth's environment.

Human geographers analyze population trends, theorize social and cultural change, interpret geo-political conflict, and seek to explain the geography of human economic activities around the world. Human geographers are concerned with observed distributions and analytical explanation. They invariably focus on the spatial and, whether implicit or explicit, have a great deal to say about the moral and political dimensions of human activity.

Human beings are the heartbeat of a country. Human capital—an intangible asset—decides the use of tangible and material resources to fulfil the objectives of any society. Since people constitute the most significant resource of any country, human development becomes critical for its socio-economic progress. Human resources in terms of demographic trends are important, as also the development of human resources through programmes in education, health, social welfare and science and technology.

Human resources are of critical importance for the growth of knowledge and technology, value addition and improvement of competitiveness in manufacturing through processes of continuous improvement. In fact, the human resources are the only *appreciating resources* in a manufacturing system. They are the only resources that have the motivation and ability to increase their value if suitable conditions are provided, whereas all other resources—machines, building, materials and so on—depreciate in value with time. The best enterprises view their people as their prime asset and the source of their competitive advantage. Nations that have achieved sustainable competitiveness in manufacturing even when they do not have required raw materials, such as Japan and South Korea, have created systems for the continuous improvement of the capabilities of their human resources.

Economic geography is the study of the place, distribution and spatial organization of economic activities across the world. It represents a traditional sub-field of the discipline of geography. However, many economists have also approached the field in ways more typical of the discipline of economics.

Economic geography has taken a variety of approaches to many different subject matters, including the location of industries, economics of agglomeration, transportation, international trade, real estate, and the relationship between the environment and the economy.

Environmental geography is the branch of geography that describes the spatial aspects of interactions between humans and the natural world. It is the study of systematic description of different components of environment and interactions of man with these components.

Environmental geography is the study of characteristic features of various components of the environment, the interactions between and among the components in a geo-ecosystem in terms of ecosystem of varying spatial and temporal scales.

Modinagar **Meenu Agrawal**

Part I
Human Geography

1

Demographic Transition Theory and Development and Management of Human Resources

1.1 What is Human Geography?

As an intellectual discipline, geography is divided into the sub-fields of physical geography and human geography, the latter concentrating upon the study of human activities, by the application of qualitative and quantitative research methods. Human geography is the branch of geography that deals with the study of people and their communities, cultures, economies, and interactions with the environment by studying their relations with and across space and place.

Human geography attends to human patterns of social interaction, as well as spatial level interdependencies, and how they influence or affect the earth's environment. In short, human geography is the branch of geography that deals with the study of people and their communities, cultures, economies, and interactions with the environment by studying their relations with and across space and place. Human geography is a wide-ranging discipline that draws together many of the strands important for understanding the world today. It examines human societies and how they develop, their culture, economy and politics, all within the context of their environment.

Human geography is a major sub-discipline within the wider subject field of geography. Traditionally, geography is considered the study of the Earth's environments and peoples, and the interactions between them.

Literally, human geography could be interpreted as the study of the geography of humans: when, where, and how humans evolved, developed strategies for survival, and dispersed to other parts of the world. Some within geography would indeed consider such themes important to geography. They invite analysis of how humans inhabited and related to physical environments, how humans used (and abused) resources, adapted to different climates, and developed distinct regional cultures.

Human geographers analyze population trends, theorize social and cultural change, interpret geo-political conflict, and seek to explain the geography of human economic activities around the world. Human geographers tend to explore social, economic, cultural, political, and demographic dimensions of human existence, and situate analysis in geographical space. Human geographers are concerned with observed distributions and analytical explanation. They invariably focus on the spatial and, whether implicit or explicit, have a great deal to say about the moral and political dimensions of human activity.

1.2 Importance of Human Resources

The resource base of a country consists of: (a) human resources, (b) non-renewable resources (coal, petroleum) which are an endowment of nature and whose total size gets depleted with time and (c) renewable resources (solar energy) which can be continuously created and whose base can be expanded through human efforts.

Human beings are the heartbeat of a country. Human capital—an intangible asset—decides the use of tangible and material resources to fulfil the objectives of any society. Since people constitute the most significant resource of any country, human development becomes critical for its socio-economic progress. Human resources in terms of demographic trends are important, as also the development of human resources through programmes in education, health, social welfare and science and technology.

Human resources are of critical importance for the growth of knowledge and technology, value addition and improvement of competitiveness in manufacturing through processes of continuous improvement. In fact, the human resources are the only *appreciating resources* in a manufacturing system. They are the only resources that have the motivation and ability to increase their value if suitable conditions are provided, whereas all other resources—machines, building, materials and so on—depreciate in value with time. The best enterprises view their people as their prime asset and the source of their competitive advantage. Nations that have achieved sustainable competitiveness in manufacturing even when they do not have required raw materials, such as Japan and South Korea, have created systems for the continuous improvement of the capabilities of their human resources.

1.3 Demographic Transition Theory

According to the theory of demographic transition, propounded by A.J. Coale and E.M. Hoover, every country passes through the following three stages of demographic transition.

1.3.1 First Stage: During the first stage, the economy is rural and agriculture is the main occupation of the people. Techniques of production are primitive and per capita income is low. This type of economy is characterised by high birth rate and high death rate. High birth rate is attributable to widespread illiteracy, superstitions, absence of family planning methods and deep-rooted social and religious beliefs about family size. Likewise, death rate is also high on account of lack of medical facilities, poor sanitation and malnutrition. Thus, high birth rate is balanced by high death rate, and population remains stable or increases marginally. The first stage is marked by high growth potential of population but low actual growth.

1.3.2 Second Stage: It marks the beginning of the process of economic development. Living standard of the people starts improving. In this stage, death rate declines sharply owing to improved medical facilities, particularly eradication of mass-killing diseases like smallpox, cholera and plague. However, birth rate continues to remain at high levels because social and religious beliefs about marriage and family size take much longer time to change. Hence, high birth rate and falling death rate accelerate the growth of population. This stage is termed as the stage of *population explosion*. The high growth potential of the first stage is realised in the form of high actual growth of population.

1.3.3 Third Stage: In this stage, the economy moves from an agrarian to an industrial society. There is an increasing trend toward urbanisation and small families for achieving a higher standard of living. The economy is characterised by low birth rate and low death rate. Birth rate declines due to the spread of education and family planning methods. Otherwise also, a large family is a burden in urban industrial areas. Thus, the third stage is marked by low birth rate and low death rate, resulting in stable or marginally increasing population.

These three stages of demographic transition explain the transformation of a primitive high birth and high death rate economy into a low birth rate and low death rate economy.

1.4 Human Development Defined

The notion of human well-being itself is more broadly conceived to include not only consumption of goods and services in general but more specifically to ensure that the basic material requirements of all sections of the population, especially those below the poverty line, are met and that they have access to basic social services such as health and education. Specific focus on these dimensions of social development is necessary because experience shows that economic prosperity, measured in terms of per capita income alone, does not always ensure enrichment in quality of life, as reflected, for instance, in the social indicators on health, longevity, literacy and environmental sustainability.

The ultimate objective of all economic efforts is human development which encompasses quality of life, the level of well-being and access to basic social services. The Fundamental Rights that India's Constitution guarantees to every citizen include the right to life and the right to livelihood is inherent in the right to life. In India, the emphasis on the achievement of higher economic growth along with social justice is manifest in the renewed focus on development initiatives in the social sectors.

Human development insists that everyone should enjoy a minimum level of security. In fact, a system should be built in which the State bears the responsibility for providing and ensuring an elementary or basic level of security, and leaves room for partly or wholly contributory schemes. This will mean that the responsibility to provide a floor will be primarily that of the State, and it will be left to individual citizens to acquire higher levels of security through assumption of responsibility and contributory participation.

1.5 Dimensions of Human Development

Development is the key to progress. It is measured in terms of improvement in the lives of the people and strengthening of the individual's and thereby a nation's capacity to deal with the rest of the world. Development is, therefore, interlinked with the entire social, political and cultural fabric of society. It aims at bringing about qualitative changes leading to an upward movement of the entire social system.

Development is a chain process. If one region develops, the adjoining region also develops. It gives impetus to development in all the regions that are economically connected with the adjoining region. Similarly, lack of development in one region promotes underdevelopment or slows down the pace of development in the adjoining region as well. This should be kept in mind during developmental planning.

Population explosion poses a serious threat to development. The vicious nexus between poverty and uncontrolled population is a huge obstacle in the way of achieving development objectives. Unchecked population not only slows down the pace of development but also accentuates the ecological crisis thereby preventing the benefits of development from reaching one and all. Development is a journey, not a destination. It encompasses all aspects and facets of human life from birth to death. It includes basic material needs like food, clothing and shelter to higher ones such as social, mental, intellectual, emotional and spiritual aspirations.

Development is a process. It is not an event or a happening. As a long drawn process, it may stretch over days, months, years, decades and even centuries. However, the success of a developmental initiative largely depends on the will of the nation and sincerity of its political leadership to see it through amidst all adversity.

The real objective of development, according to the United Nations Development Programme (UNDP), is to increase people's developmental choices to make development more democratic and participatory. These choices should include access to income and employment opportunities, education and health, and a clean and safe physical environment. However, enhancing the choices of one individual, or one section of society, should not restrict the choices of another. This calls for equity in human relationships.

Development is democratic. It provides equal opportunity to each and every individual to participate freely and fearlessly in all community decisions and to enjoy social, economic and political freedoms responsibly.

Development is participatory. It allows for private initiative and broad-based people's involvement at all levels—individual, local, national, international—and distributed well and benefiting all people. Development should be people-centric as it is the right of all people to individually and collectively speak their word. It is not the privilege of some few men, but the right of every man and woman.

Since participation is crucial to sharing information, knowledge, trust, commitment and right attitudes for decision-making, the development edifice needs to be woven around people, not people around development. All men, women and children must be at the centre of its attention. At the same time, development should be sustainable as raising future production may involve sacrifices made in the present.

Participation is closely linked to decentralization. It largely depends upon empowering the poor. Decentralization or the devolution of power from higher level to the ground level is the essence of democracy. Its success depends on education, accountability and designing appropriate structures and sequences of decision-making.

Thus, development is multi-dimensional. This approach to development is markedly different from the earlier approaches that regarded expansion of economic opportunities as a necessary precondition for development. Over concentration on single dimension of income alone is at best an oversimplification and at worst a gross distortion of reality because high growth rates do no automatically translate into higher levels of human development. This requires a firm policy action to forge a closer link between economic growth and human development. Just as economic growth is necessary for human development, human development is critical to economic growth. This two-way link must be at the heart of any enlightened policy action.

Therefore, income is just one aspect of the choices—and an extremely important one—but it is not the sum total of human existence. The human development index (HDI) combines national income with two social indicators—adult literacy and life expectancy—to give a composite measure of human progress. The HDI fully recognizes that the concept of human development is much broader than its measurement. Thus, development today is no longer confined to growth in gross national product (GNP) alone.

Hence, growth is not the end of development, but the absence of growth often is. Growth in numbers alone without improvement in living standards and overall quality of life is meaningless. Health, education, a good physical environment and socio-economic-political freedom to lead a free and independent life—to name a few components of well-being—may be just as important. Human development is incomplete without human freedom. Throughout history, people have been willing to sacrifice their lives to gain national and personal liberty. Thus, any index of human development should therefore give adequate weight to a society's human freedom in pursuit of material and social goals.

Therefore, development is holistic. It is comprehensive and multifaceted in approach. Real development gives precedence to enhancing human well-being over material opulence, to expanding capabilities over maximizing incomes and to enlarging freedoms over optimizing growth. All this is done by the people themselves through active participation in various processes meant to improve and enrich their lives.

Development should be sustainable. It should meet the needs of the present without compromising the ability of the future generations to meet their own needs. This kind of development has to be seen and felt in terms of improved living conditions, better infrastructure, safety and security of citizens and above all, less polluted greener environment.

1.6 Human Resources Development (HRD)

HRD aims at improving human resources. HRD is concerned with the development of competencies and effectiveness of people working in the organization. The design of HRD system should strengthens corporate planning, production processes, marketing strategies, and budgeting and finance.

Different roles in an organization should be integrated using different mechanisms, e.g. manpower planning inputs should be available to line managers so that they can do career planning. A systematic way to monitor the progress and to identify the level of effectiveness of the system is required.

HRD managers are expected to know everything about the organizational efficiency and for this they should work closely with different departmental heads in an organization. It is one of their roles to design, develop and implement the evaluation of programmes. They should assess the needs of training and development of employees, analyze the data obtained and organize further programmes for their career development.

As HRD managers are concerned about the development of their organization, it becomes their role to identify the threats and opportunities provided by the external environment, e.g. there is a strong need to bring advancement in technology based on the study of external environment. Identifying the threats and opportunities helps an organization to survive and further it helps in achieving objectives efficiently.

To manage learning is one of the most significant roles performed by HRD manager. They should communicate the results obtained from respective decision-makers so that they can take corrective action on time. It is expected that HRD managers should clearly understand the importance of career development and when it can be brought into the system of learning.

HRD managers also act as marketing specialists. They are actively involved in management function. Ultimately, their aim is to make and maintain favourable internal and external environment relations for smooth conduct of the business.

1.6.1 Skill Development: Skills and knowledge are the driving forces of economic growth and social development for any country. Countries with higher levels of skills adjust more effectively to the challenges and opportunities in domestic and international job markets. As India moves progressively towards becoming a global knowledge economy, it must meet the rising aspirations of its youth. This can be partially achieved through focus on advancement of skills that are relevant to the emerging economic environment. Government of India has recently taken a number of initiatives to empower all individuals through improved skills and knowledge to gain access to decent employment and ensure India's competitiveness in the global market.

India must invest in and build its human resources capabilities to catch up with other countries that have moved ahead and thereafter sustained competitive advantages in manufacturing. Indeed the contentious debate of *labour* versus *capital* in the enterprise could be reframed if employees are seen as assets, with value that can appreciate, rather than as labour costs. Human resources should be managed as a source of sustainable competitive advantage.

Equal access to skill development is essential for all social groups particularly women and disadvantaged section of society, to help them in securing decent employment and moving out of poverty. Removing barriers to access and addressing their specific needs are key elements in achieving inclusive growth. Entry barriers such as educational qualification, transportation, loss of wages, language etc. should be addressed. While enhancing the opportunity of skill development for all, entry assessments should be deployed to channelize people with different profiles and needs into appropriate skill development programmes.

Effort should be combined with a major initiative in raising awareness among the target groups about the benefit of skill development, employment and learning opportunities and also about support schemes that enable them to participate in training. In addition to vocational skills, the provision of soft (or life) skills—including basic literacy, numeracy, occupational safety and health, hygiene, basic labour rights, team work and confidence building—should be made as an integral component of the curricula. This will also help in empowerment of vulnerable groups.

1.7 Human Resources Management (HRM)

HRM relates to formulation of strategies by business entities concerning selection, training and rewarding of their personnel. The subject has assumed added significance in the wake of liberalization and globalization trends sweeping across the world. In the face of intense competition unleashed by market-oriented reforms, firms are vying with each other to acquire competitive advantage to prosper in business and in many cases to survive in business. Every possible strategy is being applied to achieve the explicit and implicit objectives of the firm. HRM has emerged as an important ingredient of the policy mix to score points over the existing and potential competitors.

Human beings are the heartbeat of an organization. They are the brains trust and think tanks of future strategies. Intangible assets, like human capital, decide the use of tangible and material resources innovatively to fulfil the objectives of any business entity. Vision sharing with employees with adequate empowerment constitutes an essential element of HRM strategy. A system of fair compensation for performance and provision of a good *work-life balance* and succession planning become important in the context of the *war for talent*, rising salaries and growing levels of attrition, particularly in developing economies like India.

HRM is a dynamic process of bringing people and organizations together so that the goals of each other are met. Since people constitute the most significant resource of any organization, management of human resources becomes critical for the success of the organization.

With the rapid changes in the business scenario in the recent past, organizations are forced to reorient themselves to meet the new challenges. Technological advances, global competition, demographic changes, information revolution and trends towards service society have changed the rules of the game significantly.

In such a scenario, organizations with similar set of resources can gain competitive advantage only through effective and efficient management of resources. HRM is no more an administrative function but a growth-oriented professional function. Human resources managers have to face a number of challenges for managing the modern knowledge-oriented organizations. In the light of these, several new issues have emerged including talent management, outsourcing, performance management, online recruitment, emotional intelligence, team management and impact of information technology and communications.

The premise that people provide organizations with an important source of sustainable competitive advantage is established. The effective management of human capital as a determinant of organizational performance is thus accepted. Competition, technology, management and the rise of the new economy, has forced organizations to look for innovative strategies to gain the competitive edge. The role of HRM in organizations has assumed significance in this context and has been evolving dramatically in recent years.

The successful organizations are using human resources as a strategic partner, investing them with far-reaching transformational roles and responsibilities. This activity involves making the function of managing people the most prioritized activity in the organization and integrating all policies/programmes pertaining to human resources within the framework of a company's strategy. Indian organizations are increasingly turning to HRM techniques to face the emerging challenges posed by liberalization and globalization.

HRM strategy highlights issues like talent identification, retention and engagement of employees. It has also brought out the need for a *gap analysis* and measures to fill the gaps in knowledge, talent, productivity and strategy leading to competence building and better position-person fit. A watch has to be kept on demand-supply mismatches and in-house development of multi-skilled personnel to enable companies to diversify, integrate and carry on multiple businesses. These issues call for taking new initiatives in the area of training, imparting skills and empowerment, competence mapping and career development.

Hitherto, companies in India looked at HRM as a segmented strategy. In the present context of increasing global competition, high customer expectations and emergence of novel business models, time has come when one has to revisit HRM strategy and look at it as a vital input for business. This approach involves aligning of HRM practices with business strategy and harnessing of human capital for business success. Human capital has to be deployed to secure predictable, sustainable and desirable long-term competitive advantage.

With the growing complexity of technology, customer

expectations and competitive challenges, there is need for closer industry-academia interaction and more purposeful linkage of theory and practice. Companies have to accord high priority to development of people for the development of the company. This calls for aligning aspirations of the employees with the objectives of the company.

Human resources are of critical importance for the growth of knowledge and technology, value addition and improvement of competitiveness in manufacturing through processes of continuous improvement. In fact, the human resources are the only *appreciating resources* in a manufacturing system. They are the only resources that have the motivation and ability to increase their value if suitable conditions are provided, whereas all other resources—machines, building, materials and so on—depreciate in value with time. The best enterprises view their people as their prime asset and the source of their competitive advantage. Nations that have achieved sustainable competitiveness in manufacturing even when they do not have required raw materials, such as Japan and South Korea, have created systems for the continuous improvement of the capabilities of their human resources.

India must invest in and build its human resources capabilities to catch up with other countries that have moved ahead and thereafter sustained competitive advantages in manufacturing. Human resources should be managed as a source of sustainable competitive advantage.

2

Population Trends and Characteristics: World and India

2.1 World Population, 2019

As of February 2019, the total population of the world exceeded 7.71 billion people, and this number is continuing to grow each day. However, in some areas, growth is slowing or even declining.

China is the most populous country in the world with a population exceeding 1.4 billion. It is one of just two countries with a population of more than 1 billion, with India being the second. As of 2018, India has a population of over 1.355 billion people, and its growth is expected to continue through at least 2050. By the year 2030, India is expected to become the most populous country in the world. This is because India's population will grow, while China is projected see a loss in population.

The next 11 countries that are the most populous in the world, with each having populations exceeding 100 million, are the following:

1. United States
2. Indonesia
3. Brazil
4. Pakistan
5. Nigeria
6. Bangladesh
7. Russia
8. Mexico
9. Japan
10. Ethiopia
11. Philippines.

Of these nations, all are expected to continue to grow with the exception of Russia and Japan, which will see their populations drop by 2030 before dropping again significantly by 2050.

There are many other nations that have populations of at least one million, while there are also countries that have just thousands. The smallest population in the world can be found in Vatican City, where just 801 people reside.

In 2018, the world's population grew at a rate of 1.12 percent. Every five years since the 1970s, the growth rate has continued to fall. The world's population is expected to continue to grow larger, but at a much slower rate. By 2030, the population will exceed 8 billion. In 2040, this number will grow to more than 9 billion. In 2055, the number will rise to over 10 billion, and another billion people would not be added until near the end of the century. The current annual population growth estimates from the United Nations are in the millions—estimating that over 80 million new lives are added each year.

This growth will be impacted greatly by nine specific countries which are situated to contribute to the population growth more quickly than other nations. These nations include Congo, Ethiopia, India, Indonesia, Nigeria, Pakistan, Uganda, Tanzania, and United States of America. India is on track to overtake China's position as the most populous country by the year 2030. Additionally, multiple nations within Africa are expected to fully double their populations before fertility rates begin to slow.

Global life expectancy has also improved in recent years, increasing the overall population life expectancy at birth to just over 70 years of age. The projected global life expectancy is only expected to continue to improve, reaching nearly 77 years of age by the year 2050. Important factors impacting the data on life expectancy include the projections regarding the ability to reduce AIDS/HIV impact, as well as reducing the rates of infectious and non communicable diseases.

Population aging has a massive impact on the ability of the population to maintain what is called a support ratio. One key finding from 2017 is that the majority of the world is going to face considerable growth in the 60+ age bracket. This will put enormous strain on the younger age groups as the elder population is becoming so vast without the number of births to maintain a healthy support ratio.

2.2 India: Population Trends and Characteristics

2.2.1 Importance of Census: The Indian Census—a decadal exercise—is the most credible source of information on demography (population characteristics), economic activity, literacy and education, housing and household amenities, urbanisation, fertility and mortality, scheduled castes and scheduled tribes, language, religion, migration, disability and many other socio-cultural and demographic data. Census 2011 was the 15th headcount of India's population since 1872. This is the only source of primary data in the village, town and ward level, It provides valuable information for planning and formulation of policies for Central and the State Governments and is widely used by national and international Agencies, scholars, business people, industrialists, and many more.

Delimitation/reservation of constituencies—parliamentary, assembly, panchayats and other local bodies—is also done on the basis of the demographic data collected by the Census. Census is the basis for reviewing the country's progress in the past decade, monitoring the on-going schemes of the Government and most importantly, plan for the future.

2.2.2 Population Growth: India's population has increased rapidly since Independence in 1947. The population increased from 36.1 crore in 1951 to 43.9 crore in 1961, to 54.8 crore in 1971, and to 68.5 crore in 1981. The Census of 1991 enumerated the population at 84.4 crore which rose to 102.9 crore in 2001 and was estimated at 121 crore in 2011. Thus, after China it is India that has crossed the 1 billion (100 crore) population mark. According to United Nations, *World*

Population Prospects, 2010, India's population is projected to peak at 1.718 billion (171 crore) in 2060. At its peak, India will be the most populous country in the world. China at its peak in 2025 will have 1.395 billion (139.5 crore) people. In fact, when China peaks, India will have already surpassed it in population.

Population of India increased from 103 crore in 2001 to 121 crore in 2011, an increase of 18 crore or 17.6 percent. Out of 121 crore, 62.4 crore were males and 58.6 crore were females.

More precisely, India added 18.1 crore people to its population between 2001 and 2011 against 18.2 crore in the preceding decade. However, even 18.1 crore equals the total population of Brazil, the world's fifth most populous country.

For the first time since Independence in 1947, India added fewer people to its population in the decade just ended (2001-2011) than in the previous one. While decadal population growth rates have consistently been declining since the 1960s, the absolute addition in each decade was always higher than in the previous decade. That is now changed (Table 2.1).

Table 2.1: Demographic Trends in India, 1951-2011

Period	Population at the end of the period (as on 1st March)		Per thousand population		
	Total (crore)	Urban population as percent of total population	Birth rate	Death rate	Growth rate
1951-61	43.9	17.97	41.70	22.80	18.90
1961-71	54.8	19.91	41.20	19.00	22.20
1971-81	68.5	23.34	37.10	15.00	22.10
1981-91	84.4	25.72	32.50	11.40	21.10
1991-01	102.9	27.82	27.50	9.40	18.10
2001-11	121.0	31.2	21.8	7.1	17.60

Source: Government of India, Census Reports.

Uttar Pradesh remains the most populous state (19.95

crore) followed by Maharashtra (11.2 crore) in 2011. These 2 states put together surpass US, the world's third most populous country after China and India, in population.

The unabated growth of population is attributable to a sharp decline in death rate coupled with relatively high birth rate (Table 2.1). The death rate (7.1 per thousand in 2011) has fallen due to improved health conditions, control of epidemics, better handling of famine conditions, and general improvement in the standard of living. There has been a significant decline in the infant mortality rate since Independence.

However, birth rate in India is still very high (21.8 per thousand in 2011). Many social and economic factors are responsible for high birth rate. These include universality of marriage, preference for male children, illiteracy, and poverty. The rapid growth of population has seriously hampered developmental efforts.

2.2.3 Characteristics of India's Population: These are described as under:

A. Age Composition: Age composition of population is important because it indicates the dependency ratio of the population. Dependency ratio is defined as the ratio of children below 15 years to population above 15 years. The age composition also determines the proportion of the labour force (15-60 years) in the total population. Projections of total population and its age structure are given in Table 2.2. Due to expected decline in fertility and mortality, the age structure of the population will change in the future.

B. Overall Sex Ratio: The Census also records overall sex ratio, which is the number of females to every 1,000 males across all ages. In 1921, the number of females per thousand males was 955. There were many reasons for excess of male over female population. The lack of pre-natal and post-natal care was the major cause of high death-rate among women in reproductive age. The evil practice of female infanticide in some parts of the country during British rule also contributed to reduced share of female population in total population.

Table 2.2: Projections of Age Structure of India's Population

(million)

Year	2006	2011	2016	2021	2026
Total	1112 (100.0)	1193 (100.0)	1269 (100.0)	1340 (100.0)	1400 (100.0)
Below 15 years	357 (32.1)	347 (29.1)	340 (26.8)	337 (25.1)	327 (23.4)
15-64 years	699 (62.9)	780 (65.4)	851 (67.1)	908 (67.8)	957 (68.3)
Above 65 years	56 (5.0)	66 (5.5)	78 (6.1)	95 (7.1)	116 (8.3)

Figures in parentheses are percentages of respective totals.
Source: Government of India, *Economic Survey*, 2006-07, p. 215, Table 10.7 (excerpted).

Even during the post-Independence period, the trend of sex ratio in India has been in favour of masculine population. According to the 1991 census, there were 927 females per thousand males. As per 2001 Census, the sex ratio stood at 933 females per 1,000 males, a marginal improvement over 1991. The persistent tendency towards low sex ratio can be attributed to lack of attention and care given to female children, sex selective female abortions, and the higher death-rate among women in the reproductive age. It is noteworthy that in Western countries, the sex ratio favours the feminine population.

Improved medical technology, education and improvement in quality of life during the first decade of the 21st century resulted in the overall gender ratio improving from 933 in 2001 to 940 in 2011. This is in line with general improvement in the overall sex ratio since 1991. Only 3 major states showed a decline in their sex ratio; J&K, Bihar and Gujarat.

Delhi and Haryana are the states with the worst overall sex ratios (866 and 877 respectively). In fact, a healthy sex ratio remains largely a southern phenomenon. Kerala is the only state where women outnumber men (1,084 females for every 1,000 males). Next in order is Tamil Nadu with 995 females for every 1,000 males.

C. **Child Sex Ratio (0-6 years):** The data shows that the sex ratio for children below 6 years (i.e. number of girls for every 1,000 boys) dropped from 927 in 2001 to a dismal 914 in 2011 (Table 2.3). This decline is unabated since 1961 Census. Among big states, Chhattisgarh has the highest child sex ratio of 964 followed by Kerala with 959. Haryana is at the bottom (830) followed by Punjab (846). This gender bias draws attention to a lingering societal flaw which economic growth is not being able to correct.

Table 2.3: Recent Trends in Sex Ratio and Child Sex Ratio (0-6 years) in India

Year	Sex Ratio	Child Sex Ratio
1991	927	945
2001	933	927
2011	940	914

Source: Census of India, 2011.

As a result of this declining sex ratio, millions of girls/women are missing in India. It is an alarming scenario and if this trend continues, violence against women would increase and there would be forced polyandry. The demographic balance would be permanently damaged.

One of the reasons for the declining sex ratios is the incidence of sex selection, and or sex determination followed by sex selective abortions. This constitutes a grave form of discrimination against women as women are affected as being part of a social class. This is not a pro-life or pro-choice issue. A woman's right to abortion has to be upheld on grounds of promoting women's rights to equality. The right to abortion is the right to abort any foetus. The abortion of a female foetus following a sex determination test is an act of discrimination. As this act of discrimination cannot be committed without the active intervention of medical professionals, it is essential to strictly enforce laws directed towards regulating the practice of medical professionals. However, keeping in mind the pressures that a woman is subjected to for bearing a male child, the implementation and enforcement of such laws should not lead to the further victimization of women.

The laws regulating sex determination and abortions are provided for in the Pre-conception and Pre-natal Diagnostic Techniques (Prohibition of Misuse) Act and the Medical Termination of Pregnancies Act, 1971. In addition, penal provisions on "causing miscarriages" are also provided in Sections 312-316 of the Indian Penal Code.

Sex determination before birth is widely prevalent. Certain districts in Punjab and Haryana account for a substantial drop in the decennial child sex ratio. Richer districts tend to account for a larger decline in the child sex ratio. The incidence of the use of sex determination techniques tends to be more in the most modern and developed districts. This calls into question the argument that the market economy undermines patriarchal authoritarian and male-biased traditional attitudes and spreads egalitarian values. Policy has to address the concern that inculcation of the values of market economy seems to be only enhancing gender inequity as reflected in the female foeticide and infanticide indicators.

There are two important issues of policy associated with this decline in the child sex ratio. One is the obsession with population control, which assumes that all the failures in development can be mono-causally linked to population explosion. The other more recent issue is the intrusion of the two child norm into the Panchayati Raj Acts of many states, despite its absence from the Population Policy of 2000, leading to disqualification of many elected representatives. Most of the excluded belong to the scheduled castes (SCs) and scheduled tribes (STs). Some experts have suggested a link between the imposition of the two-child norm and sex selective abortions. Imposition of the two-child norm, then, cannot be the route to population stabilisation, for it may lead to a disturbingly unbalanced population.

The two-child norm implies that the State promotes two children per family and has a system of incentives and disincentives/punishments for achieving it. A two child norm has the potential to cause immense harm to women's health in the existing social situation where son preference is high and women's status is very low. One of the gravest risks includes increase in sex selective abortion and consequent reduction in the numbers of girl children. The compulsion to have no more than two children would result in increased female foeticide. This happened in China when Government declared that no couple should have more than one child. There are lessons to be learnt from the Chinese experience.

There are two important issues of policy associated with the decline in the child sex ratio. One is the obsession with population control, which assumes that all the failures in development can be linked to population explosion. The other more recent issue is the intrusion of the two child norm into the Panchayati Raj Acts of many States, leading to disqualification of many elected representatives. Most of the excluded belong to the SCs and STs. Some experts have suggested a link between the imposition of the two-child norm and sex selective abortions. Imposition of the two-child norm then cannot be the route to population stabilization, for it may lead to a disturbingly unbalanced population.

In spite of claiming ourselves to be an ancient civilized and cultured society, it is found that even in many well educated and wealthy families, female child is not welcomed with open arms. Unfortunately, the new technology is being used to perpetuate gender bias. For example, in recent past, pre-natal diagnostic centres have mushroomed throughout the country which help in determining sex of the foetus that enable people to choose to abort female foetus. Indian parents still believe that having a daughter is like watering someone else's field.

The tentacles of pre-natal diagnostic centres are no more confined to urban areas and cities. "Mobile killer clinics" have reached even to remote rural areas.

Unfortunately, sex ratio keeps getting worse in India: it is shocking to note that in spite of the average figure of 927 girls for 1,000 boys, it puts India right at the bottom of the chart internationally. According to the report, only China with 832 girls per 1,000 boys ranks below India on this dubious front.

Ironically, the deficit of woman is more noticeable in the urban than the rural population—a factor which is frequently attributed to male migration from rural to urban areas. The deficit has now percolated down to the rural areas as well indicating an overall decrease of woman in the country. The district analysis of the child sex ratio in rural areas calculated from the 1991 census shows that there are only 42 districts, making up 10 percent of the country, where the sex ratio is in favour of girls. Of these, 31 districts like 2 in Tamil Nadu, 1 in Kerala, and 11 out of 12 in Punjab, where there are less than 900 girls to 1,000 boys.

D. Life Expectancy: Life expectancy at birth or longevity is an overall indicator of the economic and social well being of the people. As a society advances, the life expectancy of its people also increases.

Life expectancy in India at birth stood at 67.9 during 2010-14. The life expectancy has improved after Independence owing to decline in infant mortality, control of epidemics, and general improvement in the standard of living. Life expectancy of both males and females is projected to increase in the coming decades.

Increasing longevity will inevitably bring in its wake increase in the prevalence of non-communicable diseases. The growing number of senior citizens in the country poses a major challenge and the cost of providing socio-economic security and healthcare to this population has to be met. Currently, several region and culture-specific innovative interventions to provide needed care to this population are underway and among these are efforts to reverse the trend of break up of joint families. If these efforts succeed, it will be possible to provide necessary care for rapidly increasing population of senior citizens within the resources of the family and the country.

Majority of the people in their sixties will be physically and psychologically fit and would like to participate both in economic and social activities. They should be encouraged and supported to lead a productive life and contribute to the national development. Senior citizens in their seventies and beyond and those with health problems would require assistance. So far, the families have borne major share in caring for the elderly. This should remain the ideal method. However, there is growing number of elderly without family support. For them, alternate modes for caring may have to be evolved and implemented.

E. Literacy Rate: Literacy is an important factor in judging the quality of population. Illiteracy is widespread in rural areas as compared to urban areas. Therefore, concerted efforts are needed to direct literacy programmes towards rural areas with particular emphasis on female literacy.

The census definition of literacy is the ability to both read and write in any language. The population below 6 years is not counted as they are considered illiterate irrespective of their ability to read or write.

India's literacy rate for people aged 6 and older increased to 74 percent nationwide in 2011, from 65 percent in 2001. However, this was well short of the target set by the Planning Commission to achieve a literacy rate of over 85 percent by 2011-12.

Kerala has the highest literacy rate at 94 percent while Bihar the lowest at 64 percent.

For males, literacy rate rose to 82.2 percent in 2011 from 75 percent in 2001. For females, it went up to 65.5 percent in 2011 from 54 percent in 2001.

In fact, the gap in literacy between men and women got reduced to an all-time low of just 16.7 percentage points in 2011. In 2001, this gap was 21 percentage points.

Data of Census 2011 affirms the India growth story—population growth slowing down and the number of literates growing, especially female literates. The census definition of literacy is the ability to both read and write in any language. The population below 6 years is not counted as they are considered illiterate irrespective of their ability to read or write.

F. Degree of Urbanisation: Urbanisation is directly associated with economic development. In fact, a shift of population from rural to urban areas is an indicator of economic development. The shift of population to urban areas was slow during British rule, signifying that the process of economic development itself was slow during that period. Urban population which formed 10 percent of total population in 1911, moderately increased to 14 percent in 1941. This was in sharp contrast to the urbanisation trend taking place in Europe.

India ranks poorly among the countries of the world in respect of degree of urbanisation. The share of urban population in total population was 25.7 percent in 1991 which increased to 27.8 percent in 2001. In 2011, it was 31.2 percent. With prospect of industrialisation and the consequent migration of rural population to urban areas, the trend toward urbanisation will gain momentum.

As the proportion of the urban population continues to grow, investments in urban infrastructure for the provision of services such as roads, water supply and sewerage, urban transportation and the like will need to be much higher than they have been in the past.

Like many other demographic changes, urbanization has both positive and negative effects. Cities and towns have become the engines of social change and rapid economic development. Urbanisation is associated with improved access to education, employment, and healthcare, resulting in increase in the age at marriage, reduction in family size and improvement in health indices. As people have moved towards and into cities, information has flowed outward. Better communication and transportation now link urban and rural areas both economically and socially creating an urban-rural continuum of communities with improvement in some aspects of lifestyle of both.

The ever increasing reach of mass media communicates new ideas, points of reference, and available options are becoming more widely recognized, appreciated and sought. This phenomenon has affected healthcare, including reproductive health, in many ways. For example, radio and television programmes that discuss gender equity, family size preference and family planning options are now reaching formerly isolated rural populations. This can create demand for services for mothers and children, higher contraceptive use, and fewer unwanted pregnancies, smaller healthier families and lead to more rapid population stabilisation.

However, the rapid growth of urban population also poses some serious challenges. Urban population growth has outpaced the development of basic minimum services. Housing, water supply, sewerage and solid waste disposal are far from adequate. Increasing waste generation at home, offices and industries, coupled with poor waste disposal facilities result in rapid environmental deterioration. Increasing automobiles add to air pollution. All these have adverse effect on ecology and health. Poverty persists in urban and peri-urban areas. Awareness about the glaring inequities in close urban setting may lead to social unrest. As a consequence cities are facing the problem of expanding urban slums.

G. Density of Population: Density of population means the average number of persons living per squire kilometre of area. The density of population has increased steadily from 117 persons in 1951 to 216 persons in 1981, to 274 persons in 1991. It increased from 325 persons in 2001 to 382 in 2011, an increase of 17.5 percent. Since density of population indicates the land-man ratio, it is clear that this ratio has been declining over the years.

3

Population, Economic Growth and Demographic Dividend Hypothesis

Population growth and its relation to economic growth has been a matter of debate for a long time. The early Malthusian view was that population growth is likely to impede economic growth because it will put pressure on the available resources, result in reduction in per capita income and resources. This, in turn, will result in deterioration in quality of life.

Contrary to the Malthusian predictions, several of the East Asian countries have been able to achieve economic prosperity and improvement in quality of life in spite of population growth. This has been attributed to the increase in productivity due to development and utilization of innovative technologies by the young educated population who formed the majority of the growing population. These countries have been able to exploit the dynamics of demographic transition to achieve economic growth by using the human resources as the engine driving the economic development. Improved employment with adequate emoluments has promoted saving and investment which, in turn, stimulated economic growth.

3.1 Population as a Retarding Factor in Economic Growth

Unabated growth of population in India has offset to a significant extent the fruits of economic growth and used up part of the potential savings which could have been utilized to raise capital per head and the productivity of the labour force at a faster pace.

The present size and the growth rate of India's population is a drag on available economic resources. It is hindering the development process and defeating the twin objectives of removal of poverty and unemployment. The pressure of population is being felt in a variety of ways.

3.1.1 Population and Per Capita Income: A strong relationship exists between population and per capita income: Per capita income = National income/population. Economic development is generally defined in terms of increase in real per capita income. The high growth rate of population has depressed the increase in per capita income in India.

3.1.2 Population and Food Supply: The rapid increase in India's population has called for tremendous efforts to augment food supplies. In spite of the remarkable increase in foodgrains production over the years, shortages are felt in different parts of the country and rationing system is continuing and being strengthened in backward districts of the country.

3.1.3 Population and Land-Man Ratio: The pressure of population has adversely affected the land-man ratio. The growing pressure of population has also led to sub-division and fragmentation of holdings. The widespread disguised unemployment in the agricultural sector is also indicative of the burden of population on land.

3.1.4 Population and Unemployment: An increase in population is invariably accompanied by an increase in labour force. The growing unemployment in India reflects the failure of the economy to absorb the net additions to the labour force. Given the present backlog of unemployment, the continuing increase in population will further aggravate unemployment situation in the years to come.

3.1.5 Population and Basic Amenities: Unabated growth of population has exerted great pressure on the demand for basic amenities of life such as housing, and medical and educational facilities. Considerable resources are being diverted to meet basic needs of the teeming millions. This has adversely affected the availability of resources for developmental projects.

3.1.6 Population and Environment: Rapid population growth is leading to environmental deterioration. Developed countries are less densely populated and contribute very little to population growth. However, they cause massive ecological damage by the wasteful, unnecessary and unbalanced consumption the consequences of which are adversely affecting both the developed and the developing countries. In India, continued population growth has resulted in pressure on land, fragmentation of land holding, shrinkage of forests, and loss of plant and animal species.

Effective measures to reduce the rate of growth of population are imperative and must command priority of action. Apart from the expansion of family welfare services, sustained improvement in education and healthcare facilities and improved status of women in social and economic life are essential for the success of the family welfare programme and voluntary acceptance of the small family norm.

3.2 Demographic Dividend Hypothesis

Presently, India is one of the youngest nations in the world with more than 62 percent of its population in the working age group (15-59 years), and more than 54 percent of its total population below 25 years of age. Its population pyramid is expected to bulge across the 15-59 age group over the next decade. It is further estimated that the average age of the population in India by 2020 will be 29 years as against 40 years in USA, 46 years in Europe and 47 years in Japan. In fact, during the next 20 years the labour force in the industrialized world is expected to decline by 4 percent, while in India it will increase by 32 percent. This poses a formidable challenge and a huge opportunity. To reap this demographic dividend which is expected to last for next 25 years, India needs to equip its workforce with employable skills and knowledge so that they can contribute substantively to the economic growth of the country.

India is midway through its demographic dividend—a period of time when demography gives economic growth a boost by expanding the working-age share of the population. To exploit this dividend and meet the growing aspirations of those entering the labour force, India's economy needs to create enough *good jobs*—jobs that are safe and pay well, and encourage firms and workers to improve skills and productivity.

If the massive population of India is properly educated and trained, it can prove a boon for the national economy. India's demographic dividend is essentially due to two factors: (a) declining birth rates and (b) improvement in life expectancy. The declining birth rate changes the age distribution and makes for a smaller proportion of population in the dependent ages and for relatively larger share in the productive labour force. The result is low dependency ratio which can provide comparative cost advantage and competitiveness to the economy. Moreover, the global economy is expected to witness a skilled man power shortage to the extent of around 56 million by 2020. Thus, the *demographic dividend* in India needs to be exploited not only to expand the production possibility frontier but also to meet the skilled manpower requirements of India and other countries.

Thus, in the longer run, there is another important potential strength arising from India's demographic trends. Dependency rate (ratio of dependent to working age population) is falling whereas that of industrialised countries and even China is rising. The presence of a skilled young population in an environment where investment is expanding and the industrial world ageing could be a major advantage. It is, however, important to realise that we can only reap this demographic dividend if we invest massively on human resource development and skill formation and create an economic environment capable of absorbing our relatively young working population in productive employment.

This demographic dividend can add to growth potential, provided two conditions are fulfilled. First, higher levels of health, education and skill development must be achieved. Second, an environment must be created in which the economy not only grows rapidly, but also enhances good quality employment/livelihood opportunities to meet the needs and aspirations of the youth.

It was earlier assumed that population growth during demographic transition will lead to overcrowding, poverty, under-nutrition, environmental deterioration, poor quality of life and increase in disease burden. Experience in the last few decades has shown that this may not always be correct. India is currently in the phase of demographic transition when the increase in population is mainly among younger, better educated and healthy population with low morbidity and mortality rate. The challenge for the health sector is to promote healthy life styles, improve access to and utilisation of healthcare so that the country can achieve substantial reduction in mortality and morbidity.

Occupational health and environmental health programmes need be augmented to ensure that working population remain healthy and productive. If these challenges are fully met, it is possible to accelerate reduction in morbidity and mortality rate in this age group and improve health indices of the country.

With growing number of senior citizens there may be substantial increase in healthcare needs especially for management of non-communicable diseases. Increasing availability and awareness about technological advances for management of these problems, rising expectations of the population and the ever-escalating cost of healthcare are some of the problems that the healthcare system has to cope with. Healthcare delivery systems will have to gear up to taking up necessary preventive, promotive, curative and rehabilitative care for growing population of senior citizens.

4

Urbanization and Rural-Urban Co-ordination

Urbanization is a key indicator of economic development and should be seen as a positive factor for overall development. As an economy grows, its towns and cities expand in size and volume. Urbanization is a natural consequence of economic changes that take place as a country develops. At the same time, urbanization helps to contribute to the growth process at large. This is manifest in the increasing contribution of urban sector to national income.

4.1 Urbanization and its Effects

The process of urbanization has gathered considerable momentum in recent times and this has put urban infrastructure and services under severe strain. For example, several cities in India have only two to four hours of water supply during the entire day. Smaller cities, because of inadequate financial resources, have found it particularly difficult to cope with the increasing demands on services.

The positive role of urbanization is often over-shadowed by the evident deterioration in the physical environment and quality of life in the urban areas caused by widening gap between demand and supply of essential services and infrastructure. This results from increasing population, pressure on urban centres, most of which are financially and organisationally ill-equipped to respond to infrastructural needs. Public investment in urban infrastructure has also been less than adequate. The challenge of reorienting the urbanization process, thus, lies in overcoming the infrastructural deficiencies and taking the best advantage of economic momentum inherent in urbanization.

4.1.1 Positive Effects of Urbanization: Like many other demographic changes, urbanization has both positive and negative effects. Cities and towns have become the engines of social change and rapid economic development. Urbanization is associated with improved access to education, employment, and healthcare, resulting in increase in the age at marriage, reduction in family size and improvement in health indices. As people have moved towards and into cities, information has flowed outward. Better communication and transportation now link urban and rural areas both economically and socially creating an urban-rural continuum of communities with improvement in some aspects of lifestyle of both.

The ever increasing reach of mass media communicates new ideas, points of reference, and available options are becoming more widely recognized, appreciated and sought. This phenomenon has affected health care, including reproductive health, in many ways. For instance, radio and television programmes that discuss gender equity, family size preference and family planning options are now reaching formerly isolated rural populations. This can create demand for services for mothers and children, higher contraceptive use, and fewer unwanted pregnancies, smaller healthier families and lead to more rapid population stabilisation.

4.1.2 Negative Effects of Urbanization: However, the rapid growth of urban population also poses some serious challenges. Urban population growth has outpaced the development of basic minimum services. Housing, water supply, sewerage and solid waste disposal are far from adequate. Increasing waste generation at home, offices and industries, coupled with poor waste disposal facilities result in rapid environmental deterioration. Increasing automobiles add to air pollution. All these have adverse effect on ecology and health. Poverty persists in urban and peri-urban areas. Awareness about the glaring inequities in close urban setting may lead to social unrest. As a consequence cities are facing the problem of expanding urban slums.

4.2 Rising Urbanization in India

Urbanization is directly associated with economic

development. In fact, a shift of population from rural to urban areas is an indicator of economic development. The shift of population to urban areas was slow during British rule because the process of economic development itself was slow during that period. Urban population which formed 10 percent of total population in 1911, moderately increased to 14 percent in 1941. This was in sharp contrast to the urbanization trend taking place in Europe.

India ranks poorly among the countries of the world in respect of degree of urbanization. The share of urban population in total population was 25.7 percent in 1991 which increased to 27.8 percent in 2001, as per Census 2001.

About 377 million Indians comprising of about 31 percent of the country's population, live in urban areas according to Census 2011. This is a smaller proportion compared to other large developing countries, for example, 45 percent in China, 54 percent in Indonesia, 78 percent in Mexico and 87 percent in Brazil. With the more rapid growth of the Indian economy in recent years, which is expected to continue, the rate of urbanization will increase. Projections are that by 2031, about 600 million Indians will reside in urban areas.

4.2.1 Concentration of Urban Population: There is a concentration of the urban population in large cities and existing urban agglomerations. As per Census 2011, there are 53 million plus cities accounting for about 43 percent of India's urban population. Class-I cities with population over 3 lakh accounted for about 56 percent of the urban population and with a population ranging from 1 lakh to 3 lakh accounted for another 14 percent. This pattern of population concentration in large cities reflects spatial polarisation of the employment opportunities. While it is expected that gains from an agglomeration economy would lead to some polarisation of economic activities, there is a need for developing an optimal portfolio of cities by drawing regional development plans and promoting growth centres that are employment intensive and consistent with the economic potential including the natural endowment of cities and regions.

The availability of water to provide for the needs of a large urban population must be a critical factor in plans for urban development.

Though the proportion of urban population concentrated in larger cities continues to remain high, there is some evidence that other urban growth nodes are emerging underscoring the need for adequate policy attention to smaller cities and peri-urban areas as against the narrow focus of concentrating on large cities. Census 2011 notes that the number of towns in India increased from 5,161 in 2001 to as many as 7,935 in 2011.

An accelerated pace of urbanization would imply significant spill over of existing cities into peri-urban areas. As borne out by a recent study by the World Bank—*India Urbanization Review: Urbanization beyond Municipalities* (2012) already there are evidences that peri-urban areas in the vicinity of large cities are centres of intense economic activities. A large number of new towns are 'born' in the vicinity of existing cities with million plus population. If these trends are any indication of how the future will unfold, much of India's urbanization challenge will be to transform land-use and expand infrastructure in its largest cities and neighbouring suburbs.

Jobs and people are flowing from metropolitan cores to nearby settlements—regardless of whether they are classified as urban or rural often giving rise to haphazard urbanization in the peri-urban areas. The challenge is to ensure that new cities and existing metropolises are connected and land-use change is coordinated with infrastructure development to accommodate urban redevelopment and urban spatial expansion.

4.2.2 Inter-State Variations in Urbanization: There is wide variation among states in urbanization. At one end of the spectrum is the National Capital Territory of Delhi, with 93 percent of its population living in urban areas. At the other end, Himachal Pradesh is the least urbanised state with only 9.8 percent of its population in urban areas. Tamil Nadu is the most urbanised among the larger states with 43.9 percent urban population, followed by Maharashtra with 42.4 percent and

Gujarat with 37.4 percent. Among the larger states, Bihar has the lowest proportion of urban population (10.5 percent), below Assam (12.7 percent) and Odisha (14.9 percent). Pattern of population concentration in large cities reflects spatial polarization of employment opportunities.

4.2.3 Consequences of Rising Urbanization: Rising urbanization in India has led to tremendous pressure on civic infrastructure systems, water supply, sewerage and drainage, uncollected solid waste, parks and open spaces, transport etc. It has also led to deterioration in the quality of city environments. In several cities, the problems of traffic congestion, pollution, poverty, inadequate housing, crime, and social unrest are assuming alarming proportions. Further, growing urbanization is characterized by incomplete devolution of functions to the elected bodies, lack of financial resources, unwillingness to progress towards municipal autonomy, adherence to outdated methods in property taxation, hesitation in levy of user charges, unsatisfactory role of parastatals in the provision of water supply and sanitation services etc.

As the proportion of the urban population continues to grow, investments in urban infrastructure for the provision of services such as roads, water supply and sewerage, transportation and the like will need to be much higher than they have been in the past.

The likely increase in urban productivity and population due to the new economic policies of the Government of India will place a heavy demand on all kinds of urban infrastructure and services. The infrastructure bottlenecks in urban centres are likely to pose serious impediments in enhancing the productivity.

Rising urbanization has increased the functional responsibilities of municipalities. To meet the scale and challenge of urbanization, municipal governments are always looking for additional funds from various sources.

Since a significant part of national income originates in urban areas, efforts must be made to maintain and enhance urban productivity which, in turn, depends on the level and quality of urban infrastructure. The demand for urban infrastructure services has increased, and is likely to accelerate further, due to rising personal incomes, rapid growth of population, and general increase in economic activities. Inability of municipal governments to meet the rising demand would adversely affect growth prospects of the economy.

Urbanization will be central to India's strategy of achieving faster and more inclusive growth because agglomeration and densification of economic activities (and habitations) in urban conglomerations stimulates economic efficiencies and provides more opportunities for earning livelihoods. Thus, urbanization increases avenues for entrepreneurship and employment compared to what is possible in dispersed rural areas. It, thereby, enables faster inclusion of more people in the process of economic growth.

4.3 Features of Urban Infrastructure Services

Urban infrastructure services have the following features:

1. Most urban infrastructure services are natural monopolies and their marginal cost declines over a very large range of output. As such, it is feared that the private sector might exploit the monopolistic situation. Such services include water, waste water management, telephone, electricity, bridge, and road networks.
2. Many services like sanitation and solid waste disposal (SWD) have significant external economies. As a consequence, market-based systems may fail to provide the service in adequate quantity and quality.
3. It is difficult to exclude anyone from using certain public services like roads or street lighting. The consumer may refuse to pay for the service since he may be able to use it free of charge legally or otherwise.
4. Certain infrastructure services being necessities (like water) have almost inelastic demand. Private provision of these could result in exploitative pricing unless prices are regulated.

5. Requirement of heavy investment in capital equipment discourages private sector entry into certain infrastructure segments.

The above mentioned characteristics have for long been used as valid arguments for blocking entry of the private sector into infrastructure. The arguments, however, are slowly losing their validity due to many technological and organizational innovations. Unbundling of services has been a major mechanism through which the misconception about the economies of scale argument has been overcome. Technological innovations in the areas of sanitation and sewerage have permitted low-cost supply options. Increasing range and quality of service has reduced the cost of providing the service, making the operation commercially viable and also opening up areas for private sector operations. The recognition of the demand aspect has made remunerative pricing possible in some segments.

By and large, governments have not been very effective suppliers of many services. The cost of government failures has been much higher than the possible cost of market failure. Commercialisation of infrastructure projects basically means efficient provision of service to the consumers' satisfaction on cost-recovery basis. Since the public sector in most cases is an inefficient provider due to its inherent characteristics, promotion of privatisation itself becomes an instrument for commercialisation.

4.4 Functions of Local Bodies

Functional responsibilities of local bodies vary from country to country and within a country. Still some common patterns are discernible. Broadly speaking, the functions of a local body (e.g., a municipality) can be divided into the following three categories.

4.4.1 Essential Civic Functions: The main function of a municipality is to provide and maintain core (or essential) civic services. These include: refuse collection, street lighting, water supply, sewage disposal, fire protection, abattoirs, and primary health services. These are services for which decision-making rests with the municipalities.

4.4.2 Regulatory Functions: These functions pertain to regulation of industry, trade and construction activities. Municipalities issue licences, permits and levy fees of various kinds, and also impose fines for violation of rules and regulations. Charges for regulatory functions should be so fixed as to cover at least the cost of administration and surveillance. If these services are subsidised it would put strain on resources.

4.4.3 Agency Functions: These are functions (e.g., protection of environment) which are funded out of State revenues by specific transfers.

4.5 Financing of Local Bodies

In the public finance literature, the following general rules are mentioned as regards the financing of local bodies.

1. Where the benefits of a local public service are measurable and accrue to readily identifiable individuals/households within a jurisdiction, user charges are the most appropriate method of financing the service.
2. Local public services which are services to general public in the sense that identification of beneficiaries and measurement of benefits to individuals/households is difficult, should be financed by taxes on local residents. Such services include traffic control, street lighting, security, and general administration.
3. Services the benefits of which spill over to neighbouring jurisdictions should be financed by intergovernmental transfers. These services include health, education, anti-pollution measures, and other social welfare activities.
4. Long-term borrowings are the appropriate source to finance capital projects with long-term gains.

Higher level governments generally assign certain taxes to local bodies to augment their resources. Tax literature suggests following principles for assignment of taxes to local bodies.

1. Municipal governments should be assigned those taxes that are leviable on bases which are *immobile* or *location-specific* and those whose burden cannot be exported outside the municipal jurisdiction. Property tax is a case in point.
2. Local tax base should be easily identifiable and its incidence transparent.
3. Tax yield should be stable, predictable, and buoyant.
4. Rate schedule of the tax should possess a reasonable degree of progressivity.
5. The tax should be easy to administer.

Based on the foregoing considerations, the following taxes are generally assigned to local bodies: (a) property tax, (b) entertainment tax, (c) tax on professions, (d) tax on advertisements and (e) octroi/tolls.

In India, urban infrastructure services are provided by local level agencies. Funds have generally been in the form of loans/grants from the Central and State Governments. Own resources of urban local bodies (ULBs) have been insufficient even to meet the O&M requirements of these services. Since most urban infrastructure services have been treated as public services and the concept of cost recovery has never been considered relevant, a commercial approach to these services has not developed. Even if the facilities were funded by loans, the repayment of loans generally took adjustments or paid out of grants made by State Governments. Even when user charges are levied, the price per unit is too low to cover even the variable cost of providing the service.

The fact that infrastructure services do not pay for themselves, and the government does not have the financial capacity to continue to subsidise the beneficiaries, has resulted in low availability of funds. With increasing requirements, this has meant deficiency in volumes as well as quality of service. Consequently, a parallel unorganised sector for provision of many of these services has developed, resulting in high prices and qualitatively deficient services. From a societal point of view, these are expensive solutions. It is high time that a commercial approach is adopted.

In order to augment resources in the urban infrastructure, 100 percent foreign direct investment (FDI) has been permitted in the development of integrated township since 2001. However, investments have not materialised because of very rigid existing conditions relating to land procurement especially in urban areas. Moreover, there are problems relating to lack of clear titles, old protective tenancy and rent control. The system of maintenance of land records need to be improved through computerisation. This, together with rationalisation of stamp duty, would make things easier for those interested in entering into partnership for development of townships.

In terms of financing patterns, the foundation of urban infrastructure has to be user charges. It is possible for urban institutions to access funds from the capital markets to finance a large portion of capital expenditure on urban infrastructure, which can be serviced by user charges in the future. While municipal bond issues have indeed taken place, the magnitude of resources raised is as yet insignificant. The user-charge financed approach can facilitate a massive increase in capital expenditure on urban infrastructure without worsening the fiscal problem. In addition, the tariff restructuring or subsidy design allows for more efficient and targeted impact on the poor.

4.5.1 Cost Effectiveness: The major demands of the strategy to minimise cost should be technological appropriateness, proper attention to maintenance, curbing misuse of services and efficient institutional arrangements for providing services. To promote cost effectiveness, different infrastructure projects may be packaged together like water supply and drainage projects. Coordination between different departments providing different services will also reduce overall cost of production.

The supply orientation in infrastructure policy has not succeeded to respond adequately to the evolution of demand. A commercial approach requires that demand-orientation service should be supplied in response to demand rather than in anticipation of demand. This will also improve cost recovery and financial viability of such projects.

4.5.2 Innovations for Better Urbanization: Managing India's ongoing urbanization will place huge requirements on financial as well as human resources in the country. Given the scarcity of resources in the medium term, innovation will have a significant role to play. It is critical to promote innovation and research in several ways.

Given the huge requirement of funds, it is critical to incentivise cost reducing innovations in the fields of materials and processes. The support can be in the form of incubation assistance and low cost funds. Incentives could be in the form of recognition and rewards.

Creating innovative solutions is not enough. These solutions need to be spread across the country to maximise impact.

4.5.3 Pooled Finance Development Fund (PFDF): Direct access to capital markets for funding urban infrastructure projects, often leveraging government grants, is an established option in global markets. However, capital market investors require well structured projects with a clear understanding of inherent risks, appropriate pricing of such risks, and an established system for ensuring timely payment of dues.

In this context, the Government of India launched the Pooled Finance Development Fund (PFDF) scheme. The PFDF scheme is meant to provide credit enhancement grants to a pool of (primarily) medium and smaller municipalities to enable them to access the capital market through pooled finance municipal bonds for investment in urban infrastructure projects. The PFDF scheme is meant for creation of essential municipal infrastructure, with priority on water and sanitation projects. In case access to the PFDF scheme is being sought for projects in other areas, it must be first demonstrated that adequate service quality exists in the water and sanitation sectors in areas under the jurisdiction of the respective municipalities. The main objectives of the PFDF scheme are four-fold:

1. Facilitate ULBs to access the capital and financial market for investment in essential municipal infrastructure.
2. Facilitate development of bankable urban infrastructure projects.
3. Reduce the cost of borrowings to local bodies with appropriate credit enhancement measures and through restructuring of existing costly debts.
4. Facilitate development of municipal bond market.

4.5.4 Tax Free Municipal Bonds: In 2000-01, the Government inserted a new clause (vii) in Section 10(15) of the Income Tax Act, 1961, exempting interest income from bonds issued by local authorities. Funds raised from tax free municipal bonds are to be used only for capital investments in urban infrastructure for providing one or more of the following:

1. Potable water supply.
2. Sewerage or sanitation.
3. Drainage.
4. Solid waste management.
5. Roads, bridges and flyovers.
6. Urban transport (if this is a municipal function under respective state legislation).

Ministry of Urban Development, Government of India was designated as the nodal agency for processing applications for issue of tax free bonds.

Guidelines were issued by the Ministry of Urban Development on February 8, 2001 for regulating issue of tax free municipal bonds. Under the guidelines, such bonds will be issued for raising resources for capital investment in creation of new infrastructure as well as augmentation of existing systems.

Guidelines for issue of municipal tax free bonds were revised in consultation with the Ministry of Finance and circulated to all the State Governments and UT Governments on March 7, 2006.

Municipal bonds were successfully issued by several municipal corporations like, Bangalore, Ahmedabad, Nagpur, Nasik, and Madurai for raising resources for urban infrastructure.

4.6 Municipal Commercial Borrowings

In India, Plan allocations of Central and State Governments are the chief source of financing capital projects of municipal governments. Other sources of finance include: (a) internal resources of municipalities, (b) institutional resources (HUDCO etc.), and (c) multilateral agencies.

The scope for additional funds from Central and State Governments is limited in view of the pressing need to reduce fiscal deficit. Similarly, institutional finances at low cost are unlikely to be available in the wake of financial sector reforms. Under such circumstances, municipal authorities should be permitted access to the capital market to mobilise additional resources. Recent expansion and modernisation of capital market in India suggests that inflow of capital into equity and debt market is quite high if attractive rate of return is offered.

4.6.1 Rationale for Municipal Commercial Borrowings: It is both fair and efficient that projects with long-term benefits are financed through long-term borrowings. If long-term capital projects are financed out of current revenues and/or short-term borrowings, the future generations would enjoy free-riding. Since the benefits of a capital project are reaped over a long period of time, i.e. by more than one generation of tax payers, the financing of such projects should place the repayment burden on the present as well as future generations.

4.6.2 Factors Determining Success of Municipal Bonds: To attract a share of capital market for municipalities, the following conditions need to be satisfied.

1. Urban infrastructure projects should be commercially viable.
2. Municipal bonds are rated by some recognised credit rating institution. This will help build confidence of investors in the bond issue as well as help in its subsequent trading on the secondary market.
3. Such bonds should carry tax concessions.
4. Revenues accruing to the municipal entity are sufficiently elastic.

5. Security behind the debt taken by the municipal entity is sound.
6. Municipal entity makes provision for the creation of debt-servicing funds and the legal procedures for seeking recourse in the event of default.
7. Municipal entity is competent to pledge revenues for debt-servicing and extend collateral in terms of commercial property, plant and machinery and other assets.

4.6.3 Limitations: Municipal access to capital market, though desirable, is hindered by a variety of factors which may be classified into two categories: (a) restrictions imposed by the higher level government, and (b) other constraints.

The Constitution of India imposes various types of restrictions on the borrowing powers of the State Governments which, in turn, impose restrictions on the borrowing powers of the municipalities under them. Since borrowings by the lower level government are guaranteed, in most cases, by the higher level government, the latter has a right to impose such restrictions. These restrictions apply to: (a) type of debt, (b) amount of debt, (c) term of the debt, and (d) use of debt funds. Approval of the higher level government, which is often cumbersome, is needed before the debt is floated.

Thus, no municipal authority can borrow without an explicit sanction of its State Government. When the loan amount exceeds ₹ 25 lakh or the repayment period is over 30 years, local borrowings need Central approval under the provisions of the Local Authorities Loan Act, 1914 (a Central Legislation).

Among the 'other constraints', the more important are the following: Low credit worthiness of municipalities, their poor tract record as borrowers, and lack of trustworthy financial intermediaries.

Despite the foregoing hurdles, some municipalities in India have successfully tapped the bond market.

4.7 Privatisation of Municipal Services

The scope for privatisation of some municipal services in

order to reduce costs is a moot question.

Municipalities alone cannot handle huge infrastructural projects like water supply, sewage disposal, and urban transport. Involvement of central, state, and private sector is required to meet the scale of investment needed in these areas. Similarly, greater participation of private sector is desirable in the provision of civic services, particularly those the consumption of which can be attributed to individuals and households. There are many types of arrangement in respect of public-private-partnership depending on situation. However, care should be taken not to dilute current social commitments while embarking on public-private partnership.

The historical and ideological resistance to private sector participation persists in most places. Consequently, few local bodies have tried out private sector participation in civic services on any significant scale. Wherever it has happened, the experiment has remained limited to disposal of solid wastes, and maintenance of parks.

The disenchantment with utility enterprises of municipalities is not conceptual but borne out of their inefficient and sometimes corrupt management. The merits of privatisation are seen in terms of improvement in efficiency and reduction in the budgetary burden of state-owned enterprises.

Though the need for private sector participation is widely felt, it is not openly expressed. Very rarely political parties have spoken publicly against the public sector. Contrarily, there is a stiff opposition by political parties to any move to undermine the importance of public sector. The strong unions of public sector enterprises come in handy for politicians to prevent the erosion of state and municipal activities.

4.8 Urban Governance

Urban governance today is characterised by fragmentation of responsibility, incomplete devolution of functions and funds to the elected bodies and urban local bodies (ULBs), unwillingness to progress towards municipal autonomy, adherence to outmoded methods of property tax and reluctance to levy user charges. State Governments continue to take decisions on such matters as rates of user charges, property tax, octroi, role of parastatals in water supply and sanitation services etc., with little reference to the ULBs that are affected by these decisions.

Far from strengthening the constitutional role of the elected ULBs, such developments only reinforce the perception that ULBs are subordinate entities under the day-to-day control of the State Governments, beholden to them not only for the development of the cities but often for their very survival. There appears to be a lack of confidence that many of the ULBs are capable of meeting their obligations as institutions of local self-governance. In the present set up, initiatives for local developmental activities rarely come from the ULBs. Experience shows that functional autonomy becomes a reality only when it is accompanied by financial independence. State governments, therefore, need to strengthen the autonomous functioning of the ULBs through positive measures, and in particular, ensure their financial self-reliance.

The key urban concern is the growing gap between demand and supply of basic services. While there has been a steady growth in the housing stock, infrastructure and services, the gaps between demand and supply have been rising, even in terms of conservative norms.

Since overall government resources are limited and must be applied to other priority sectors such as health and education, it is necessary that cities, especially the larger ones, and progressively even the smaller ones, are encouraged and enabled to draw resources from the market and the private sector. For this, they must improve their governance and ability to implement projects. They will also have to manage their land resources more strategically, both to ensure better land use and to secure what will be a principal resource for their future financial needs. They must become able to recover adequate service charges, and equitably, from their inhabitants, which will require them to demonstrate an ability to deliver better and more reliable services.

In short, urban governance is very weak, with poor co-ordination amongst the many agencies that must work together to create and maintain good functioning habitats. Personnel and institutional capabilities for urban management have to be developed on a massive scale across the country. Capabilities for planning locally are woefully inadequate, which is leading to projects not aligned with local priorities and poor coordination amongst separate initiatives.

Information technology (IT) can play an important role in improving governance. With municipal administration becoming increasingly complex, the benefits of IT adoption are becoming more visible across several municipalities. E-governance must be a mandatory reform under the renewed Jawaharlal Nehru National Urban Renewal Mission (JNNURM) and its implementation should be required in all cities receiving assistance under the capacity building component of the Mission. A major constraint in full fledged transition to e-governance is lack of a suitable national level architecture. This has led to States and ULBs independently developing e-governance platforms which are often mutually incompatible. This has also prevented States from replicating successful architecture developed in other States leading to avoidable expenditure. To address this problem, the Ministry of Housing and Urban Affairs should finalise a suitable national level architecture with sufficient flexibility for customization at the State and ULB level.

4.8.1 Building Capacity for Managing Urbanization: Lack of sufficient capacity across all levels of Government is a root cause of India's urban development challenges. Many States have lagged in programme utilisation due to inadequate capabilities of governance and management. Traditionally, capacity building, though critical, has been given low priority, which is evident in the absence of dedicated municipal cadres and robust urban management structures. Substantial skill gaps exist across almost all areas of urban management. This is driven as much by the lack of credible and specialized supply side institutions as it is by poor demand from those responsible for urban management in cities. Addressing the capacity deficit must be a key endeavour.

E-governance initiatives including online project management information system should be implemented across all ULBs. There should be a State-level nodal agency for implementation and monitoring of all e-governance initiatives within the State. It should also identify the training needs and coordinate with relevant agencies to conduct trainings.

4.9 Urban Planning

A key weakness of India's urbanization efforts is that the agenda is being implemented through disjointed projects/activities with inadequate or no planning for the urban area as a whole. The Master Plan approach generally focuses on only the core area of the city, has little linkages to any financial and operating strategy and, in many cases has been used as a regulatory tool instead of being a blue print for development of dynamic and smart cities. A master plan typically freezes the land use pattern and building bye-laws and so on determines the permissible limits of floor space index (FSI) and minimum setback areas. Often these provisions do not take into account the potential of the city to grow, especially where trunk infrastructure has been laid. This results in sub-optimal use of land as well as the infrastructure.

Absence of any long-term plan prevents development of 'good cities' in which all the parts of the system—urban services, transportation, housing, commercial activities—fit together harmoniously. Planning must be holistic before it is detailed, for example, urban housing and urban poverty issues cannot be separated from other aspects of urban planning. Holistic planning, even if not detailed, is required at the local urban level, at the metropolitan level and at State and national levels too.

Urban planning is a key determinant of demand for mobility: whether it is a compact city where the various functions—residential and commercial, services, education and recreation—are located and how they interconnect; whether public transport is available for newly developed areas etc. City governments should be made accountable for greenhouse gas emissions caused by poorly planned suburban sprawl.

Low rise and higher density is a way to improve the overall energy efficiency of urban areas. General urban consolidation and more intensive mixed use of local activity centres close to public transport nodes provide opportunities to lower carbon emissions.

The planning of housing areas can significantly affect living comfort during heat waves. Innovative cooling systems contribute to limitation of emissions.

Planting trees around buildings to shade urban surfaces and green roofs to reduce their temperature lead to substantial reductions in energy consumption for air conditioning and sequester carbon while growing. Trees to shade roads and parking lots reduce evaporative emissions from gasoline, which contribute to increased levels of urban ozone. Biomass from trees and shrubs can be used as wood energy to replace fossil fuels, thus contributing to climate adaptation.

Planners should take into account specific effects of climate change while planning for a district/region. Some issues which need to be tackled at the regional level include flexible management of resources, including allocation of water, preservation of threatened areas.

Sound urban practices lead to long-term sustainability. The National Commission on Urbanization (NCU) India (1988) recommended low-rise high density (LRHD) built form for Indian cities. It stated that such a form is less expensive to maintain and has other advantages like equity. According to NCU, income profile and affordability suggest that a range of small and medium-sized plots, between 50 square metres and 100 square metres (with some plots perhaps up to 200 square metres) can satisfy the needs of over 95 percent of the urban population. NCU felt that this typology is more economical than apartments because less space is required for public circulation and lifts, besides it also provides much better living conditions. According to NCU, a 50 square metres plot per family with 5 members would generate a net density of 1,000 persons per hectare (i.e. a gross residential density of 500 persons per hectare). Similarly, a 100 square metres plot would generate a gross residential density of 250 persons per hectare. It also stated that high gross densities in the inner city can be tackled by interventions in the city structure and by adjusting land use allocation within the city itself to create spaces for social overheads. Its recommendations for built form specified that residential sites should be provided so that:

1. 50 percent of the land is in plots between 25 and 100 square metres.
2. 25 percent of the land is in the plots between 100 and 200 square metres.
3. 25 percent of the land is either in this size of plots or any other sizes.

NCU further stated that as long as Indian cities remain within stipulated density thresholds (i.e. neighbourhood densities of 250 to 1,000 persons per hectare) there are efficient and cost-effective solutions within available resources. The densification can be increased at selected nodal points depending on the holding capacity of the area. Densification should be related to the mass public transport network.

High population density aggravates negative externalities like air pollution, noise and loss of green space. However, it may improve accessibility of services, reduce per capita domestic energy consumption and also promote infrastructure efficiency and use of public transport.

In general, advantages of densification can be summarized as follows: (a) protection of the countryside, green space and biodiversity, (b) reduction of travel distance, emission of green house gases and thus global warming, (c) reduction in use of material for construction of infrastructure, (d) economies of scale in providing social and institutional services like hospitals, banks etc. and (e) better interactive community life.

The disadvantages are as follows: (a) overcrowding, (b) traffic congestion, (c) ill health, (d) crime and (e) high energy demand in compact high rise buildings.

Arriving at an optimum form would require a balance between densification and expansion.

4.10 Urban-Rural Co-ordination

Attention needs to be focussed not only on the growing challenges of urbanization but on the relationship between urban and rural development. The rapid transformation in the country's urban scenario must be taken into account and provided for, in order that urban growth becomes compatible with healthy socio-economic development of the nation. It will be necessary to take note of the prevailing dichotomy in rural and urban development and evolve a mechanism for bringing about rural-urban cohesion in the management of growth. This can be achieved through the process of spatial planning, which is an integrating concept that makes it possible to achieve the composite development of human settlements while stimulating economic growth.

The rural hinterland has played a critical role in sustaining urbanization. This is reflected in the indicators of sources of primary inputs, competitively priced labour for urban economic activities, primary funds as reflected in comparative urban and rural credit-deposit ratios and market for urban products. However, the unending migration of the rural poor to urban areas may have a destabilising effect on urbanization and its sustainability. Income and employment opportunities will have to rise in the rural areas, through both the farm and non-farm sectors and habitats and basic services have to be improved so that with rural development and congenial habitats, rural areas emerge as sustainable centres of economic activities and human settlements.

In a country still largely rural and agricultural in character, it is natural that programmes for agricultural and rural development should receive the greatest emphasis, in particular those for rural employment creation and assistance to the rural poor. Urban development should, however, be seen as complementary to rural development and policies affecting the process of urbanization should be such as to strengthen the links between towns and cities and their hinterland. Urban areas of all sizes operate as market centres for agricultural output and provide a variety of service functions in addition to operating as centres of manufacturing activity. These functions should be strengthened such that towns and cities serve the rural areas more effectively.

The process of urbanization should then be seen as aiding employment and income generation in rural areas rather than as a competitive process. Larger towns serve as distribution centres for seed, fertilisers and credit for farmers as well as serving as organised markets for their produce. The bigger cities provide services and facilities to both the smaller towns as well as rural areas in their hinterland. Thus, national policy on urban development should view the whole range of urban settlements as having a role to play in the national development process.

It is also important to view the provision of services in rural areas in an integrated manner. Availability of shelter, safe water supply and facilities for hygienic sanitation are as necessary in the rural areas as in the urban. Owing to different residential densities, however, different technologies can be used in different sizes of settlements in providing these services.

It is only through purposive public programmes providing essential services like water and sewerage along with low cost shelter programmes like sites and services that the urban landscape of the country can be improved to enable the urban population to function more efficiently. Particular attention must be paid to the functioning of the small, medium and intermediate cities in order to aid them in their role as market centres and as suppliers of goods and services for agriculture. The environmental and infrastructural conditions in some of these towns and cities have been neglected so long that their efficient functioning is beginning to be hampered.

Although the theme of a *rural-urban divide* still colours some policy discourse in India, there is a growing recognition that urbanization is necessary to realise India's growth potential, and that rural-urban linkages must be strengthened. Indeed this will accelerate growth of the rural sector also.

The fortunes of the agricultural sector are crucially linked to the manner in which growth in the industry and services sectors unfolds. People living in rural areas typically tap the opportunities that cities provide for employment, entrepreneurial avenues, and education. As urbanization grows, demand for food items other than foodgrains, i.e. vegetables, lentils, milk, eggs and so on, also grows. This leads to investments in infrastructure, logistics, processing and packaging in rural and peri-urban areas. Such investments and other economic inter-linkages connect and build synergy between rural and urban centres. Thus, the rural sector also benefits from good management of neighbouring urban conglomerations.

4.11 Major Issues in Urbanization

The concentration of urban population in a few large cities has led to tremendous pressure on civic infrastructure systems like water supply, sewerage and drainage, solid waste management, parks and open spaces, transport etc. It has also led to deterioration in the quality of city environment. In several cities, the problems of traffic congestion, pollution, poverty, slums, crime and social unrest are assuming alarming proportions. Climate change is likely to exacerbate the existing stresses that these settlements already face. It may also impact measures that are being undertaken for sustainable development of these areas.

Attitudes to urban growth within the country tend to swing

between two extremes. Cities are seen either as an unavoidable evil or in a more positive way as *engines of growth.* The former view is held by those who focus on the growth of slums and squatter colonies, the congestion on the roads and environmental degradation. The others, in contrast, focus on the bustling formal and informal sectors in urban areas and their contribution to the economy, the diversification of occupations away from traditional land-based ones to newer forms of production and services, and the lower levels of poverty as compared to rural areas. From this point of view, the moderate pace of urbanization in the country has been a cause of disappointment. There is, however, no rural versus urban conflict either in terms of national growth, or in development priorities.

Good urban governance calls for adequate policy and legal frameworks, the existence of regulatory and planning authorities, human skills, a sound revenue base, accounting and accountability. Substantial work has already been done to upgrade the urban infrastructure and several parastatals and urban development authorities have acquired considerable skills in planning and executing projects. In particular, parastatal agencies and bodies such as development authorities need to play a supportive role to the elected bodies rather than taking over functions which properly belong to the ULBs. The objective of devolution and decentralisation should be carried forward by making parastatals and authorities partners and agencies of the democratically elected ULBs, thus making a gradual transition to local management while continuing to use the expertise of the organisations set up and supervised by the State Governments.

A large part of civic amenities, particularly water supply, sanitation and sewerage, are managed with assets that have outlived their operational efficiency. The required massive upgradation and renovation of these assets, is constrained by high population density and concentrated commercial activities at the locations where these service assets are installed. The lack of comprehensive urban planning in the past to promote regular upgradation and renewal has resulted in a large backlog of development activities.

Another crucial aspect requiring immediate attention is that physical infrastructure assets created in urban areas have generally been languishing due to inadequate attention and/or improper O&M. The fiscal flows to the sector have laid emphasis only on the creation of physical assets. Not much effort has been made either to manage these assets efficiently or to achieve self-sustainability. It is, therefore, necessary that a link be established between asset creation and management, as both are important components for ensuring sustained service delivery.

To sum up, India is a part of the global trend towards increasing urbanization. Cities hold tremendous potential as engines of economic and social development, creating jobs and generating wealth through economies of scale. They need to be sustained and augmented through the high urban productivity for country's economic growth. National economic growth and poverty reduction efforts will be increasingly determined by the productivity of these cities and towns. For Indian cities to become growth oriented and productive, it is essential to achieve a world class urban system. This in turn depends on attaining efficiency and equity in the delivery and financing of urban infrastructure.

Cities and towns are emerging as centres of domestic and international investments where most of the commercial activities take place. The higher productivity of any urban area depends on the availability and quality of infrastructure services. Urban economic activities are dependent upon urban infrastructure like roads, water supply, power, telecommunication, mass transportation and other civic infrastructure like sanitation and solid waste management. Massive urban growth has led to complex problems of inadequacy of basic urban services.

Rapid economic growth will inevitably lead to an increase in urbanization as cities provide large economies of agglomeration for individual activity. Unfortunately, the state of urban infrastructure has deteriorated to an extent that the country is not able to fully benefit from these economies. Poor urban infrastructure inflicts a severe hardship on people. Congested roads, poor public transport, inadequate availability of water, improper treatment of sewage, uncollected solid waste and above all grossly inadequate housing, all these severely decrease the quality of life and lower the well-being of urban population.

The rural-urban continuum should be strengthened so that gaps between rural and urban lifestyles are reduced. Effective urban strategies and programmes cannot be developed in isolation of those in the rural areas.

Part II
Economic Geography

5

Work Force and Classification of Economic Activity

5.1 What is Economic Geography?

Economic geography is the study of the place, distribution and spatial organization of economic activities across the world. It represents a traditional sub-field of the discipline of geography. However, many economists have also approached the field in ways more typical of the discipline of economics.

Economic geography is also defined by the geographers as the study of human economic activities under varying sets of conditions which is associated with production, location, distribution, consumption, exchange of resources, and spatial organization of economic activities across the world.

Economic geography has taken a variety of approaches to many different subject matters, including the location of industries, economics of agglomeration, transportation, international trade, real estate, and the relationship between the environment and the economy.

5.2 Labour Force and Work Force

Population, which is engaged in any economic activity (employed persons) and population seeking work (unemployed) constitute labour force. The size of labour force is determined by the number of people in the age group 15-59 years. Traditionally, children below the age of 15 and old persons above the age of 59 are excluded from the definition of labour force. Estimation of labour force is a pre-requisite to ensure optimal utilisation of available human resources. Manpower planning aims to provide adequate labour force, of appropriate skills and quality, to different sectors of the economy so that there is no mismatch between skills required and skills available.

Total population of a country may be divided into two categories: (a) working population and (b) non-working population. The size of working population or work force is important in relation to the level of economic activities. This is so because labour being an active factor of production, is the source of all wealth. The work force rate in a country depends on factors such as age composition, sex ratio, attitude toward work, and availability of employment opportunities. Apparently, these factors differ from country to country.

Labour force participation rate (LFPR) is obtained by dividing the number of persons in the labour force with the total population. Work participation rate (WPR), on the other hand, is obtained by dividing the number of persons in the work force with total population. Unemployment rate is obtained by dividing the number of those unemployed with the total number of persons in the labour force.

LFPR, WPR and unemployment rate are a few of the major indicators generally being used to assess labour market conditions. The decision rule by which a person is classified as belonging to labour force, work force and unemployment categories is crucial in the context of determining employment generation strategy.

The main features of the work force participation in India are the following:

1. Worker-population ratio in India is low in comparison to developed countries on account of higher proportion of child population, exclusion of unpaid family workers, and low female participation.
2. Participation rate in rural areas is higher than in urban areas. Lack of educational facilities in rural areas force people to join family work in the fields/crafts at an early age.
3. Female participation rate is much smaller than male participation rate. This is reflective of the low social status of the women in Indian society. The principal reasons for low participation by women in labour force are the

following:

- Wage rates of women are lower than for men for comparable occupations.
- Women are denied access to certain occupations, though they may be capable of doing that work as well as the men.
- Skill development of women is not uniform across all trades. Participation by them remains confined to a few labour-intensive occupations such as stitching, teaching, nursing etc.

4. Female participation rate in rural areas is higher than the female participation rate in urban areas. Women belonging to affluent families in urban areas generally do not work.

A majority of women workers in the country are employed in the rural areas, primarily as labourers and cultivators. In the urban areas, a majority of the women workers are employed in the unorganized sector, in household industries, petty trades and services, buildings and construction etc.

5.3 Occupational Classification and Occupational Structure

Occupational classification refers to the distribution of available occupations in a country into meaningful categories. In general, all occupations are broadly divided into three categories:

1. Primary sector (agriculture and allied activities).
2. Secondary sector (industrial activities).
3. Tertiary sector (services sector).

Occupational structure refers to the distribution of working persons across primary sector, secondary sector and tertiary sector.

There is a close relationship between economic development and occupational structure of a country. A higher per capita income country is always associated with a higher proportion of the working population employed in tertiary sector. Contrarily, a low per capita income country is always associated with a higher proportion of working population engaged in agriculture.

In the preliminary stage of economic growth, the

proportion of the work force engaged in the agricultural and allied occupations is high. As an economy grows, the share of working population in primary sector declines and that of secondary and tertiary sectors increases. At high levels of economic development, the share of tertiary sector is more than that of secondary sector.

5.4 Meaning and Nature of Unemployment

Economic security is one of the main components of human security. It constitutes the crux of social security in the conventional sense. Economic security requires employment and an assured source of income adequate for meeting one's basic needs.

Unemployment is a situation when willing workers fail to get jobs at the prevailing wage rates. In other words, unemployment means involuntary idleness. From social point of view, unemployment means wastage of the precious labour resources of the country. For an individual, unemployment is a painful and demoralising experience. Employment to be gainful and sustainable has to be productive in character.

The problem of unemployment is common to all countries—advanced as well as industrially backward—although the causes and extent of unemployment differ from country to country. Three main types of unemployment, distinguished according to causes, are the following:

1. Unemployment arising from deficiency in aggregate demand.
2. Unemployment arising from shortage of capital equipment or other complementary resources.
3. Frictional unemployment.

The first type is mainly cyclical in character and has been recurring in almost all developed countries from time to time. The second is found mainly in under-developed countries, while the third may occur in any type of economy. The goal of social policy in all countries has been to achieve full employment by directing investments along certain channels and by encouraging capital formation.

In under-developed countries, production is carried on with insufficient amount of real capital per head of population. In almost all processes of production and distribution, the techniques are relatively backward leading to various forms of unemployment—seasonal unemployment in agriculture, and disguised or even manifest unemployment in certain industries and services.

There is need to view the employment situation not only in the aggregate but also in its distinct urban and rural components. In assessing the size of the problem, it is necessary to take into account its magnitude in the urban and rural sectors in different regions of the country. It is necessary further to distinguish the educated unemployed from other unemployed persons.

5.4.1 Urban Unemployment: Urban unemployment may be classified into two categories:

- Industrial unemployment.
- Educated unemployment.

Industrial unemployment is the result of slow growth of industrial development vis-à-vis growth of labour force. Lately, there has been a tendency for the rural people to migrate to cities in search of employment. This has led to further competition in the job market.

Another facet of urban unemployment is the lack of job opportunities for the educated people. University degree holders and even professionally trained people are finding it difficult to get jobs. Unemployment among the educated is mainly due to over emphasis on theoretical aspects of various subjects. The education system is cut-off from ground realities of the Indian economy.

Further, employment in urban areas is linked with fluctuations in the state of business, transport and industry. Any change in conditions is reflected in an increase or decrease in employment figures.

5.4.2 Rural Unemployment: Unemployment in the

agricultural sector is the most serious aspect of unemployment problem. First of all, there is open unemployment among the landless agricultural workers. With the decline of cottage industries and handicrafts, the rural population has no alternative means of livelihood. They have to fall back on the agricultural sector which is already overcrowded. There is also considerable disguised unemployment in the agricultural sector. It means more people are engaged in agricultural operations than required. In technical language, the marginal productivity of many hands in the agricultural sector is zero. Yet another dimension of rural unemployment is the problem of seasonal unemployment. Agriculture by its very nature is a seasonal activity. For a significant part of the year, farmers are out of work. In the absence of supplementary sources of employment, they have to remain unemployed during slack agricultural season.

In the rural areas, both unemployment and under-employment exist side by side—the distinction between them is by no means sharp. In the villages, unemployment ordinarily takes the form of under-employment. In many parts of the country, during the busy agricultural seasons, shortages of labour are frequently reported, but over the greater part of the year, a large proportion of agricultural labour and others engaged in allied activities are without continuous employment. The consequent drift of workers from villages to towns only serves to shift the focus of attention from rural to urban areas. Urban and rural unemployment in fact constitute an indivisible problem.

5.5 Manpower Planning

Economic policy should lay emphasis on harnessing India's abundant human resources and improving their capabilities for development. An important aspect of human resources development relates to the development of manpower needed for the fulfilment of the targets of growth of different sectors of the economy. Manpower planning should ensure the proper linkage of economic planning with manpower and educational planning so that no plan programme suffers from a lack of trained manpower that is needed. The problems in this regard are likely to be different for the rural and urban sectors and for the organised and the unorganised labour force. In each case, the development of skills ought to address itself to the task of generating the appropriate categories of skills in keeping with the level of technology, the local environment and the development process.

It has been noticed that alongside surpluses in certain manpower categories, there are critical shortages for certain other categories, and sometimes for specified disciplines under broad categories. In this connection, efforts to bring the development of different skills in line with social needs would involve adequate attention to working conditions, real earnings and incentives so as to counter the market forces, which reflect the existing income distribution and cause imbalances in skill formation.

In other words, the relative earnings of each category should be commensurate with the comparative benefits to the economy from their services and should broadly reflect their relative usefulness for meeting the socio-economic needs of the country. In order to avoid imbalances, especially of trained and educated manpower, the existing training programmes would have to be reviewed.

The traditional skills of rural artisans require upgradation in tune with the changing village culture. Fuller utilisation of the already available manpower through the upgradation of skills and on-the job training/retraining would be necessary. Training facilities will have to be organised for categories of manpower where critical shortages have been identified and in the formation of new skills which are emerging.

The growth process should generate greater productive work opportunities by concentrating on sectors, sub-sectors and technologies which are labour-oriented, and in regions characterised by higher rates of unemployment and under-employment. Recognising the high incidence of under-employment and increasing casualisation of labour, there is a need to enhance employment opportunities for the poor, particularly for those who are in seasonal occupation.

6

Agriculture, Animal Husbandry, Forestry and Fishery

6.1 Agriculture

The cultivation of land, including horticulture, fruit growing, crop and seed growing, dairy farming and livestock breeding. The use of land to raise crops for eating first started about 10,000 years ago. All plants grown for food have been developed over many centuries from wild plants, which have been progressively bred to give the best yields in different types of environment. Genes from wild plants are likely to be more hardy and resistant to disease, and are still kept in gene banks to strengthen new cultivated varieties.

Agriculture is the science and art of cultivating plants and livestock. Agriculture was the key development in the rise of human civilization, whereby farming of domesticated species created food surpluses that enabled people to live in cities.

Modern agronomy and technological developments have sharply increased yields, while causing widespread ecological and environmental damage. Selective breeding and modern practices in animal husbandry have similarly increased the output of meat, but have raised concerns about animal welfare and environmental damage. Environmental issues include contributions to global warming, deforestation, and growth hormones in industrial meat production. Genetically modified organisms are widely used, although some are banned in certain countries.

Agriculture, specifically farming, remains a hazardous industry, and farmers worldwide remain at high risk of work-related injuries, lung disease, noise-induced hearing loss, skin diseases, as well as certain cancers related to chemical use and prolonged sun exposure. On industrialized farms, injuries frequently involve the use of agricultural machinery, and a common cause of fatal agricultural injuries in developed countries is tractor rollovers. Pesticides and other chemicals used in farming can also be hazardous to worker health, and workers exposed to pesticides may experience illness or have children with birth defects. As an industry in which families commonly share in work and live on the farm itself, entire families can be at risk for injuries, illness, and death.

Ages 0-6 may be an especially vulnerable population in agriculture; common causes of fatal injuries among young farm workers include drowning, machinery and motor accidents, including with all-terrain vehicles.

International Labour Organization considers agriculture "one of the most hazardous of all economic sectors". It estimates that the annual work-related death toll among agricultural employees is at least 1,70,000, twice the average rate of other jobs. In addition, incidences of death, injury and illness related to agricultural activities often go unreported. The organization has developed the Safety and Health in Agriculture Convention, 2001, which covers the range of risks in the agriculture occupation, the prevention of these risks and the role that individuals and organizations engaged in agriculture should play.

6.1.1 Sectors and Sub-sectors of Agriculture: These are as under:

A. Crop Sector: Being the largest sector in agriculture, crop sector holds a large number of contributors, viz. field crops, plantation crops and horticultural crops. This sector constitutes the backbone of the India's food economy

(a) Field Crops: These include the following:

- Cereals (paddy, wheat, barley, maize, gram and other cereals).
- Pulses (gram, blackgram, moth, other pulses).
- Oilseeds (linseed, sesame, groundnut, mustard, soyabean, sunflower, rapeseed).
- Fibres (cotton, jute, mesta and others).
- Sugarcane.

(b) Plantation Crops: These include the following:

- Tea, coffee, tobacco, opium, betel leaves, saffron, cocoa, rubber, coconut, cashew.
- Condiments and spices (cardamom, chillies, black pepper, turmeric, cumin, fenugreek, tamarind, cloves, nutmeg). Some of these crops constitute important items of India's exports. India is the largest producer, processor, consumer and exporter of cashew in the world. Coconut is an important tree crop grown extensively in coastal areas providing livelihood to about 10 million people in cultivation, processing and related activities.

(c) Horticultural Crops: These consist of the following;

- Fruits (banana, mango, grapes, papaya, apple, orange and others).
- Vegetables (potato, onion, tomato, radish, carrot, green peas, and others).

B. Livestock: It consists of the following: (a) milk, meat, eggs, (b) wool and hair, (c) silkworm and honey cocoon and (d) dung.

C. Forestry: This sector is composed of: (a) industrial wood, (b) firewood and (c) non-timber forest products.

D. Fisheries: It comprises: (a) inland fish and (b) marine fish.

Cropping systems vary among farms depending on the available resources and constraints, geography and climate of the farm, government policy, economic, social and political pressures, and the philosophy and culture of the farmer.

Shifting cultivation (or slash and burn) is a system in which forests are burnt, releasing nutrients to support cultivation of annual and then perennial crops for a period of several years. Then the plot is left fallow to re-grow forest, and the farmer moves to a new plot, returning after many more years (10-20). This fallow period is shortened if population density grows, requiring the input of nutrients (fertilizer or manure) and some manual pest control. Annual cultivation is the next phase of intensity in which there is no fallow period. This requires even greater nutrient and pest control inputs.

6.2 Animal Husbandry/Livestock

Animal husbandry is the breeding and raising of animals for meat, milk, eggs, or wool), and for work and transport. Working animals, including horses, mules, oxen, water buffalo, camels, donkeys, and dogs, have for centuries been used to help cultivate fields, harvest crops, wrangle other animals, and transport farm products to buyers.

Livestock plays an important role in the lives of the people across the globe. Livestock provides stability to family income especially in the arid and semi-arid regions of a country and is an insurance against the vagaries of nature due to drought, famine and other natural calamities. Major part of the livestock population is concentrated in the marginal and small size of holdings.

Livestock sector not only provides essential proteins and nutritious human diet through milk, eggs, meat etc., but also plays an important role in utilization of non-edible agricultural by products. Livestock also provides raw material/by products such as hides and skins, blood, bone, fat etc.

Market opportunities have opened up for the livestock sector following the economic liberalization. However, the sector's ability to capitalize on new market opportunity is constrained by the availability and quality of support services. Moreover, these services are not available at the doorsteps of the producers. There is a need to restructure service delivery mechanism to become conducive to the requirement of the rural livestock producers. Lack of credit for livestock production has been a major problem. Public sector lending is very low. The strategy should be to correct these distortions and ensure timely availability of inputs and services including credit to livestock farmers.

Livestock activities engage women in much larger proportion. The ownership of livestock is much more egalitarian since poor farmer families mostly own cattle, buffalo, sheep and goats. The major constraints experienced by farmers relate to breed, fodder, feed, healthcare and remunerative prices for their produce. There is a need to address these issues through an appropriate strategy. Further, to enhance the income of livestock owners, agri-clinics operated by veterinary and farm science graduates should be encouraged to improve productivity and overall efficiency of livestock. At the same time, crop-livestock mixed farming systems should be promoted, apart from encouraging production of organic manures and bio-fertilizers. Livestock insurance would also be revamped and made accessible to all farmers.

Grassland based livestock production relies upon plant material such as shrubland, rangeland, and pastures for feeding ruminant animals. Outside nutrient inputs may be used, however manure is returned directly to the grassland as a major nutrient source. This system is particularly important in areas where crop production is not feasible because of climate or soil, representing 30-40 million pastoralists. Mixed production systems use grassland, fodder crops and grain feed crops as feed for ruminant and monogastric (one stomach; mainly chickens and pigs) livestock. Manure is typically recycled in mixed systems as a fertilizer for crops.

Landless systems rely upon feed from outside the farm, representing the de-linking of crop and livestock production found more prevalently in Organisation for Economic Co-operation and Development member countries. Synthetic fertilizers are more heavily relied upon for crop production and manure utilization becomes a challenge as well as a source for pollution. Industrialized countries use these operations to produce much of the global supplies of poultry and pork.

6.3 Forestry

Forests play a vital role in social, cultural, historical, economic and industrial development of any country and in maintaining its ecological balance. They are the resource base for sustenance of its population and a storehouse of biodiversity. Other vocations of land use, such as agriculture and animal husbandry, are dependent on forests and forestlands. Forests not only maintain and improve the moisture regime and provide clean air but also produce humus and maintain soil fertility.

They provide recreation and aesthetic refreshment for people, and irreplaceable supplies of oxygen and soil nutrients. Forests clean the environment by muffling noises, buffering strong winds and trapping dust and gases. They also moderate extremes of temperature.

The significance of forests can be understood by recognizing them as the primary producers and protectors of several natural resources. Traditionally, timber and pulp are regarded as the chief economic products of forests. In modern times, economic benefits of forests are recognized also in terms of climate control, pollution abatement, and wildlife maintenance. The economic importance of non-timber forest products and efforts to evaluate them are on the rise. Forests also harbour wild medicinal plants.

Forest products include timber, bamboo, fuel wood, fodder and medicinal plants besides intangible goods and services.

Fuel wood is a major source of energy in rural as well as urban India. Referring to the high dependence of the Indian population on wood-based energy, it has been predicted that firewood would continue to be used as it is: (a) the least expensive fuel, (b) consistent with cultural patterns and living habits, (c) socially acceptable and (d) responsive to low inputs and low maintenance etc.

Theft from forest areas is largely in the form of fuel wood, partially organized by contractors and partially resorted to by villagers in large numbers in order to earn a livelihood. Enforcement of laws becomes difficult when dealing with large number of villagers, mostly women, who carry fuel wood by head loads to the towns. Dependence on fuel has to be reduced by providing alternative fuels and energy sources for cooking, heating etc. Among the most obvious alternatives is biogas for which cattle dung is the main feedstock. Another source of energy that could be tapped is solar energy, especially for cooking.

6.3.1 Forests and Agriculture: Food security is the outcome of complex interactions among natural resource management, political, social, and economic factors. Forests, as an important element within this matrix, affect food security in three major areas.

Forests help maintain favourable and stable conditions needed for sustained agricultural productivity. Moisture and nutrient leaching from the adjoining forests maintain the fertility of the agriculture fields. It is common in forest regions of Eastern India plateau (Northern Odisha, Jharkhand, and Eastern Chattisgarh) for farmers to desist from the use of chemical fertilizers. Thus, many farmers leave their fields near a moderately dense forest to be fed entirely from moisture and nutrient from the forests and save the precious cow dung to fertilize more distant fields.

Over the years, local communities have developed sophisticated indigenous techniques to augment and harvest forest-based moisture and nutrient flow. Raised bunds on forest boundaries along the contours are common in the Eastern India plateau. Further, in recent years a cash rich economy has developed in many forest areas when farmers found out that fields at the foot of the forested hills are best suited for potato cultivation, as these have accumulated rich potash deposit that has leached down from the uphill forests.

Windbreaks and shelterbelts protect crops from drying and damaging winds. Local people fully appreciate the importance of forests in disease control and prevention of epidemic outbreak related to agriculture crops. Local villagers in forested regions appreciate the role of avifauna in the control of rodent and insect pests. Forests also serve as the chief source of tree fodder for feeding livestock. Of growing importance is the role forests play as storehouses of biodiversity, potentially very important in future crop breeding and pest and disease management programmes.

6.3.2 Forests and Fisheries: Forests also have significant links with inland and marine fisheries. Rivers and streams are rich fishing grounds for local populations. Forests regulate the volume and fluctuations of stream flows and provide a shaded riparian environment favourable for the development of smaller life forms which fish feed on. Villagers in the forest region of Eastern India plateau know that the water flowing from bamboo forests has high nutrient capacity and is able to support larger volumes and healthy population of edible aquatic fauna (fish, crab, mussel, snail etc.).

The mangrove swamps in southern India provide habitats for many fish species, especially shrimps. The fish catch from these areas not only enriches protein-deficient diets and generates household income, but also helps maintain/enrich local level social capital when the whole village gathers to celebrate community fish harvesting festivals based on the principles of strict equality in sharing of the catch.

6.3.3 Forest Foods: Forest foods are important for the local villagers during both stress and normal periods, and the use of forest foods as a component of local response strategies to increasing food insecurity is widely documented. In normal times, leafy vegetables, mushroom, berries and fruits available in different seasons form the usual component of their diet. Having a diverse resource base with a range of different trees, plants and insect species, forests increase the options for maintaining food security. Different seasonal products complement each other with seasonally different pattern of availability. Leafy vegetables and fruits provide essential vitamins and minerals as dietary supplements. Similarly, wild fruits are very rich in Vitamin A and C.

Moreover, the forest foods have a definite pro-poor bias. Women and children are the largest consumers, followed by the elderly. In the wake of social customs forcing rural women to eat at the end—and at times only the left over and poor portions of the cooked meal—such harvests do help women regain some nutrition.

During the periods of acute food shortage, forest foods

sustain livelihoods.

6.3.4 Timber and Non-timber Forest Products: The supplies from natural forests have been limited following the National Forest Policy, 1988 which discourages harvesting of natural stands for commercial plantations, and the 1996 order of the Supreme Court requiring approval of the Working Plans of forests prior to its harvest.

Cash income from forests—especially non-timber forest products (NTFPs) like kendu patta, tamarind, mahua etc.—provides the buying power to purchase food when agriculture is not practiced or when crops fail. Indeed, in terms of share of total annual household income, this may not appear highly attractive in the first instance. However, a closer look reveals that since it comes at a time when income from regular sources is negligible. Thus, income from NTFP is an important factor in the earnings of the poor.

6.3.5 Fodder for Animals: In India, the fodder for animals comes from five sources:

1. Crop residues.
2. Fodder grown on grasslands, grazing on grasslands and uncultivated marginal lands.
3. Grazing on fields which are lying fallow during the dry season.
4. Fodder produced from trees and from forest areas generally.
5. Grain and other high quality feed. This is a small proportion of the total

6.3.6 Forests and Hydrological Cycle: Forests are also vital as watersheds. Due to the thick humus layer, loose soil and the soil-retaining powers of tree-roots, forests are vitally important for maintaining and regulating water flows and sub-soil water regimes. Almost all water ultimately comes from forestlands, forest rivers and lakes and from forest-derived water tables.

Water and fertile soil are the two most important prerequisites of food security. Both are irrevocably linked with forest and watershed conservation. The gravity and consequences of India's water scarcity are as yet not fully realized and hence it has not yet been universally acknowledged that the greatest product of our forests—both qualitative as well as quantitative—is water. Natural vegetation, both forests and grasslands, are the prime conservers of soil and the providers of nutrients and humus. The functional lifespan of most of our hydro-projects has been drastically reduced due to exponential siltation, caused by overuse and abuse of forests and rangelands.

India remains at the core an agrarian economy. A large portion of income of farmers still comes from water consuming crops. A burgeoning population makes an ever-increasing demand for potable water. A number of rivers emanate in mountains and crisscross its face, quenching fields and throats. It is wishful to believe that even if the mountain ranges are denuded and all vegetation is shaved off, the water will flow unhindered in the same quality and quantity. When one speaks of water regulation, therefore, the concern is wider than biodiversity or forest conservation. The concern extends to the economy and is central to the lives of the masses. Water flow, both quantitative and qualitative, may now be regarded as the single greatest product of forests, since most of our rivers and rivulets emanate from forests and forests constitute the upper catchments of these water bodies.

Other than traditional forest areas, grasslands have also several ecological imperatives. Besides providing habitat, shelter, and food, both to livestock and wildlife, grasslands also serve as important catchments for rivers, streams, reservoirs, dams, check-dams and village ponds. In short, grasslands also greatly help in the water regime and hydrological cycle of the country. Therefore, it is imperative to recognize the ecological, hydrological, economic and sociological role of grasslands as a source of survival for millions of livestock and rural people, as protectors of soil and water and of rare wildlife species and of biodiversity in general.

Forests help maintain healthy aquatic ecosystems and

provide reliable supplies of clean freshwater. Forests not only filter and clean water, but also help prevent soil erosion, reduce sedimentation in reservoirs and mitigate the risks of mudslides and floods, all problems that can threaten downstream water supplies. While forests themselves consume water, they also improve infiltration rates, thereby helping recharge underground aquifers.

The filtering capacity of the rich humus on the forest floor is critical for maintenance of many potable water sources in the country. The criticality of the contribution of forests in this respect increases in view of the fact that a large percentage of the villages in the forested region of the country still depends on traditional water sources (artesian wells, small streams etc.). Water quality is also an important aspect of forests' relation with potable water. Water coming from bamboo forests is supposedly sweeter and softer, and hence requires less energy for domestic cooking, than the water coming from sal forests.

6.3.7 Forests and Ecological Security: Forests are habitats for diverse species and hence they sustain the majority of diversity in nature. The most important benefit that the human race has been deriving from these ecosystems is the security of life-support systems. Viable populations of fauna and flora—by their interdependent collective activities—ensure that the quality of natural systems is kept at levels that maintain their life-giving quality for all life forms.

Hence, deforestation has become a major environmental concern, as it can destabilize the earth's temperature, humidity, and carbon dioxide levels.

Some of the rarest species of wildlife are found in grasslands, and many of them are totally dependent on them. The Bengal florican, one-horned rhinoceros, pygmy hog, hispid hare, wild buffalo, hog deer and the swamp deer in the terai grasslands, the great Indian bustard in dry, short grasslands, the lesser florican in monsoonal grasslands of western India, and the Nilgiri Tahr in the shola grasslands of the Western Ghats, are some examples.

Grasslands are the only breeding grounds of a number of avian species, whose nesting time is the monsoon. Due to the presence of crops in the fields, the monsoon is the period most affected by free-ranging livestock, who have nowhere else to go. This is the time when the grass grows. If grass is over-grazed at this time, it not only prevents fodder production and seed formation, but nests of ground-living birds are also trampled. No grasslands, however resilient, can bear the overuse and abuse that they are subjected to today in this country.

6.3.8 Forests and Ecotourism: Tourism, which was earlier thought to be adversary to conservation goals, is now recognized not only to be compatible but facilitative to the same. The average tourist is now better informed about the environmental impact of his travel and behaviour. Such awareness is expected to persuade people to pay more and generate a fund stream to finance conservation as well as the development of local communities. Ecotourism, as it is called, is the *mantra* of the new age travel industry. As ecotourism has mostly to do with nature and wilderness, forest departments become a key actor in the activity centred on ecotourism. Hence, the capacity of forest departments needs to be augmented, infrastructure raised and mechanisms of inter-department and inter-sectoral collaboration worked out.

6.3.9 Forests and Urban Population: While the strongest role for forestry lies in the rural context and poverty is predominantly a rural phenomenon, a substantial proportion of urban households continue to draw on the plant and animal products of forests to meet some part of their basic needs—such as construction, energy, nutrition and medicine. While the contribution of forest products will decrease as the income levels of urban households increase, many low-income families will continue to depend on wood for fuel. Similarly, for the growing numbers living in slum and marginalised communities in urban areas, gathering fuel wood may continue to be one of the few options open to them to generate income. The importance of forests to the urban poor is demonstrated by evidence that an increase in urban poverty temporarily increases demand for low cost forest products.

The other link between urban communities and forests that deserves consideration is the influence of urban markets on traded forest goods. Expanding and growing forest product activities are more likely to be found where per capita income is rising, and there is a growing demand from markets. In addition, forests also provide certain services like tourism and recreation which are used primarily by the urban population. Forests also provide ecological and environmental services of regional, national and global importance. These include watershed protection, filtering of air pollution emissions, carbon sequestration and conservation of biodiversity.

6.3.10 Sustainable Forest Management: Sustainable development has had many definitions, but the same in the case of forestry is generally understood as development involving changes in the production and/or distribution of desired goods and services which result, for a given target population, an increase in welfare that can be sustained over time. Sustainability must refer to not only maintaining and/or improving environmental quality and the productive capacity of ecosystems, but also to maintaining and/or improving the well-being of people and enhancing their capacity to utilize available resources effectively and efficiently over the long-run to meet the needs of the present and the future generations.

Forests in India can thus no longer be used in the same way now as they have been in the past and radical adjustments in managing them are required.

6.4 Fishery

Fisheries sector occupies a very important place in the socio-economic development of India. It has been recognised as a powerful income and employment generator as it stimulates growth of a number of subsidiary industries and is a source of cheap and nutritious food, besides being a foreign exchange earner. At the same time, it is an instrument of livelihood for a large section of economically backward population of the country.

Generally, fishery is an entity engaged in raising or harvesting fish which is determined by some authority to be a fishery. According to the FAO, a fishery is typically defined in terms of the "people involved, species or type of fish, area of water or seabed, method of fishing, class of boats, purpose of the activities or a combination of the foregoing features". The definition often includes a combination of fish and fishers in a region, the latter fishing for similar species with similar gear types.

A fishery may involve the capture of wild fish or raising fish through fish farming or aquaculture. Directly or indirectly, the livelihood of over 500 million people in developing countries depends on fisheries and aquaculture.

Over-fishing, including the taking of fish beyond sustainable levels, is reducing fish stocks and employment in many world regions. Fisheries can be saltwater or freshwater, wild or farmed. Examples are the salmon fishery of Alaska, tuna fishery of the Eastern Pacific, or the shrimp farm fisheries in China. Capture fisheries can be broadly classified as industrial scale, small-scale or artisanal, and recreational.

Close to 90 percent of the world's fishery catches come from oceans and seas, as opposed to inland waters. These marine catches have remained relatively stable since the mid-nineties (between 80 and 86 million tonnes). Most marine fisheries are based near the coast. This is not only because harvesting from relatively shallow waters is easier than in the open ocean, but also because fish are much more abundant near the coastal shelf, due to the abundance of nutrients available there from coastal upwelling and land run-off.

However, productive wild fisheries also exist in open oceans, particularly by seamounts, and inland in lakes and rivers. Most fisheries are wild fisheries, but farmed fisheries are increasing.

Farming can occur in coastal areas, such as with oyster farms, but more typically occur inland, in lakes, ponds, tanks and other enclosures.

7

Location of Industry

Location of industry refers to establishment of an industry or cluster of industries in a particular location or region due to availability of cheap factors of production, transport and infrastructural facilities, demand incentives, raw materials etc. These are some of the factors which attract entrepreneurs to set up their plants in a particular area. Once the process starts, it has a tendency to accelerate.

7.1 Factors Affecting Location of Industry

7.1.1 Availability of Raw Materials: This is one of the important factors in an industrial location. The mere location of industries itself may be determined by the availability or location of the raw materials.

7.1.2 Power: Power is a necessity condition for any industrial establishment. Electricity is one of the key inputs for the overall economic development of the country. The basic responsibility of the power supply industry is to provide adequate electricity at economic cost, while ensuring reliability and quality of the supply. The demand for power in both rural and urban areas is increasing rapidly.

7.1.3 Skilled Workforce: Skilled labour is important because of its contribution to enhancing productivity at the individual, industry and also national levels. Complementarities exist between physical capital and human capital on the one hand and between technology and human capital on the other. Fast changing knowledge economies call for new core competencies among all learners in the society.

7.1.4 Transport: Transport always influences the location of the industry. So the junction points of waterways, roadways and railways become humming centres of industrial activity.

7.1.5 Market: The finished goods should reach the market at the end of the process of manufacturing. Thus, nearness to the market is an important factor in the process of selecting a location for industry.

7.1.6 Water: Some industries like iron and steel, textiles and chemical require large quantities of water for their proper functioning. Such industries are established near rivers, canals, and lakes.

7.1.7 Climate: Climate of the area selected for the industry is important. Very harsh climate is a discouraging factor in the location of industry.

7.2 Alfred Weber's Theory of Industrial Location

Alfred Weber, a German economist, enunciated a systematic theory of industrial location in 1909. Weber's theory of location is purely deductive in its approach. He formulated a theory of industrial location in which an industry is located where the transportation costs of raw materials and final product is a minimum. He singled out two special cases. In one the weight of the final product is less than the weight of the raw material going into making the product.

He analyzed the factors that determine the location of industry and classified these factors into two divisions. These are as under:

1. Primary causes of regional distribution of industry (regional factors).
2. Secondary causes (agglomerative and deglomerative factors) that are responsible for redistribution of industry.

7.2.1 Primary Causes: According to Weber, transport costs and labour costs are the two regional factors on which his pure theory is based. Assuming that there are no other factors that influence the distribution of industry, except transportation costs, then it is clear that the location of industry will be pulled to those locations which have the lowest transportation costs. The key factors that determine transportation costs are as follows:

- The weight to be transported; and
- The distance to be covered.

Weber lists some more factors which influence the transportation costs such as: (a) the type of transportation system and the extent of its use, (b) the nature of the region and kinds of roads, (c) the nature of goods themselves, i.e. the qualities which, besides weight, determine the facility of transportation.

However, the location of the place of production must be determined in relation to the place of consumption and to the most advantageously located material deposits. Thus, *locational figures* are created. These locational figures depend upon: (a) the type of material deposits and (b) the nature of transformation into products.

7.2.2 Secondary Causes: We have so far been discussing primary causes of industrial location. Weber has also discussed secondary causes responsible for industrial location. He has taken into account agglomerative and deglomerative factors. An agglomerative factor, according to him is a factor which provides an advantage in production or marketing a commodity simply because industry is located at one place. On the other hand deglomerative factor is one which gives such advantage because of decentralization of production.

Agglomerative factors include gas, water etc. and are conducive for concentration of industry and deglomerative factors include land values and taxes and lead to decentralisation. Pulls of agglomerative factors are index of manufacture and locational weight. According to Weber, ratio of manufacturing cost of locational weight is co-efficient of manufacture.

According to Weber, agglomeration is encouraged with high co-efficient and deglomeration with low. According to him, we shall do well to bear in mind that labour orientation is one form of deviation from the minimum point; agglomeration to another.

When agglomerative forces appear in an industry oriented

towards labour, there takes place a competition between the agglomerative deviation and the labour deviation, a struggle to create, locations for agglomeration, as compared with labour locations, both bearing upon the foundations of the transport ground work.

8

Special Economic Zones (SEZs)

World's first SEZ was set up at Shannon in Ireland in 1958. Seven years after, India set up its first export processing zone (EPZ) at Kandla (Gujarat) in 1965, which was also the first in Asia. SEZs are seen as vehicles for inducing industrial growth in the backward regions, backward areas within a state or rural areas within a district. SEZs are linked to the idea of urban dispersal and are seen mainly as a provision of land in locations which are usually distant from the major urban centres. Usually the goal is an increase in foreign investment.

8.1 Meaning of SEZs

SEZs are geographical regions in a country subject to economic laws which are liberal than typical economic laws of that country. The word *special* mainly means special economic system and policies. A SEZ can be deemed as a *foreign territory* for the purposes of trade operations, duties and tariffs. Units in SEZs enjoy lot of fiscal pampering.

SEZs are self-contained islands providing high-quality infrastructural facilities. SEZs offer industrial, residential and commercial areas with developed plots/pre-built factories, power, telecommunications, water supply, sewerage and drainage, and educational and medical facilities.

SEZs have been established in several countries, including China, India, Iran, Jordan, Poland, Kazakhstan, Philippines and Russia. SEZs are known by different names in different countries. Some close variants of SEZs are growth centres, industrial estates, export zones, industrial parks etc. In the United States, SEZ are referred to as urban enterprise zones.

8.2 Types of SEZs

SEZs can be developed either as general SEZs, catering to

all types of industries or specialised SEZs, focusing on a specific industry, such as chemicals, automobiles or software. A specialised SEZ offers an opportunity for the industries in the zone to synergise their operations with the local industries in the region, and position themselves close to the local raw material sources. The zone can offer specific facilities such as a common effluent treatment plant, integrated design centre etc. to cater to the needs of the target industries. However, development of such a zone involves high risk and requires a longer time to sell the developed plots or pre-built factories. Therefore, a specialised SEZ is viable only in industries like information technology, plasters and textiles which are fast growing and have a large market.

SEZs are of varying sizes in terms of land occupied. A SEZ may be as small in size as 10 hectares. It can be as large as a self-contained township across thousands of hectares having airports, roads, hospitals, schools, movie theatres, shopping malls, homes and manicured parks.

8.3 Configuration of a SEZ

Normally a SEZ is divided into three zones.

1. The industrial zone encompasses industrial units catering to both domestic and export markets. It offers two options for entrepreneurs: (a) developed land and (b) pre-built factory space.
2. The residential zone houses the employees of the units. Additionally, in order to commercially exploit certain locational advantages, a portion may be developed for sale to outsiders.
3. The commercial zone provides facilities such as offices, banks, post and telecom services, shopping centres, restaurants, clubs and recreation facilities.

8.4 Advantages of SEZs

In the context of the huge demand-supply gap in infrastructure, SEZs are ideal vehicles for providing integrated infrastructural facilities. SEZs are essential for industrialisation in developing countries which, unlike the developed world, do not have uniformly good infrastructural facilities across regions. They can serve as an intermediate solution to the lack of well-developed and uniformly good infrastructural services.

SEZs have been used as engines of growth by many Asian countries such as China, Thailand, Indonesia, Malaysia and Singapore.

Following are the advantages of setting up SEZs:

1. Developed plots and pre-built factories mean that the entrepreneur can immediately set up an industrial unit without spending scarce resources in developing the necessary infrastructure and land by himself. He also saves on costs because the cost of development is spread over a large number of users.
2. SEZs can serve as catalysts for the development of surrounding region by providing opportunities for employment and creation of ancillary industries.
3. They can help develop social infrastructure like healthcare centres, educational and training facilities. They provide an opportunity to cross-subsidise development and maintenance costs of social infrastructure with surpluses from other components through a common implementing agency.
4. SEZs can be tailored to capitalise on the strengths and needs of a region such as traditional skills and industries, availability of raw materials and locational advantages. Industrial units in the SEZs can take advantage of the synergies arising from forward and backward integration with others in the same sector.
5. SEZs can also act as incubators of small and medium industries until the time these are ready to stand on their own feet.

8.5 Pre-conditions for the Success of SEZs: These can be listed as follows:

1. The location of a SEZ is the key factor determining its success. The location should be decided based on an analysis of the competitive advantage and inherent strengths of the region.
2. As foreign direct investment is very important for the success of SEZs, the foreign investment policy with reference to the SEZs should be clarified. Establishment of holding companies for investment in the SEZs should be encouraged.
3. Land acquisition by the private sector should be in tune with the policy of commercialisation of SEZs through private sector participation. In this case, terms of negotiated land purchase should be primarily determined by the market forces. The government may acquire land in exceptional cases where private sector acquisition of land is difficult and where there is a clear case for public good in the acquisition of the land.
4. Since compensation for the land acquired is often a major cause for dissatisfaction, an independent valuer should be asked to fix the price which should be related to the average of the market prices in the recent past. The government should also encourage the provision of alternative locations for displaced owners. It should be recognised that the government should assist in the land acquisition process and not fix any price.
5. The government should announce a comprehensive legal policy for SEZs based on transparency and enforceability. It is essential to recognise SEZs as infrastructure projects and provide the same incentives including tax/tariff reliefs and special dispensations that are available to an infrastructure project in the power, telecommunications or transport sector.
6. A promotional authority may be set up in each state, on the lines of bodies such as the Industrial Estates Authority of Thailand, as a one-stop agency involved in development of SEZs either by itself or through joint ventures with the

private sector. The authority should focus on monitoring and adjudicating.

7. Uninterrupted and quality power supply is a key success factor for any SEZ. State governments should encourage the supply of adequate power to the SEZs either through small captive power plants or through the support of the State Electricity Boards (SEBs) which must announce a clear policy for cogeneration so that captive power plants set up to serve SEZs can be of economic size.
8. Adequate financing through long-term debt is of critical importance for the projects. SEZs should be eligible to receive financing.
9. In order to encourage private sector financing of SEZs, financial institutions providing loans to SEZs may also be granted exemption from income tax on the profits from loans to SEZs. To encourage further investments in SEZs and also to discourage repatriation by foreign investors, tax rebate may be allowed on profits reinvested in the SEZs or in any other infrastructure project.
10. SEZs must develop connection with technological research institutions, universities, colleges and technical training institutes. Also, appropriate linkages are necessary with transportation facilities such as airports, ports, and railway terminals.

8.5.1 Possible Reasons for the Failure of a SEZ: These can be as follows:

1. Poor location of the SEZ.
2. Improper implementation and design leading to poor quality of infrastructure facilities.
3. SEZ having been built without tailoring it to the characteristics of that region.
4. Frequent changes in administrative heads and political interference.

8.6 Role of the Government

International experience indicates that SEZs need active

support from the government by way of a clear industrial policy and incentives for private sector development of SEZs.

State governments must formulate an integrated development plan for the region. In the short term, existing industrial parks should be upgraded while in the long run, a suitable policy should be identified for their commercialisation. While private sector participation in the development of SEZs would increase with time, in the medium term, the State Industrial Development Corporation (SIDCs) which hold larger pieces of land can strike an alliance with the private sector for development of SEZs.

Commercialisation requires a collaborative approach and participation from various parties including private sector financial institutions, and the state and local government. Even if the government does not opt for equity participation, it should play the role of facilitator in the project. MoU which includes a mutually agreed-upon time-table with penalties for time and cost overruns should be signed. As a partner, the government should provide an exit policy which facilitates the pullout of the private sector from a venture which turns out to be unviable. A suitable dispute redressal system would need to be designed and put in place right at the beginning of the project to facilitate smooth operation of the park after construction.

In order to facilitate speedy statutory clearances and provision of other civic facilities, the government should encourage the setting up of business support centres (BSCs) in SEZs. The BSCs should be delegated the authority to grant clearances/approvals subject to specified norms. A system of public audit should be introduced to ensure that accountability and discipline work, in respect of both the partners and that the public purpose remains secure.

8.7 Role of the Private Sector

Participation of the private sector in partnership with the government in ownership and operation of SEZs helps in the emergence of a more commercial approach. Private sector participation generally leads to the following favourable effects:

1. Competition resulting in better services and an increase in efficiency in design and focus of the SEZ, its implementation and operation.
2. Greater accountability and responsibility.
3. Professional management.
4. Use of appropriate technologies.
5. Innovation and dynamism in the design and management of the SEZ.
6. Fund mobilisation from private sector to bridge the gap due to lack of government funds.

The commitment of the project sponsors through their financial and managerial inputs, the immense opportunities for generating profits and surpluses and the competition due to an increase in the number of players would lead to proper choice of the location, design and development of infrastructural facilities.

8.8 SEZs and Small Enterprises

Very large industries are capable to acquire large tracts of land and create all necessary infrastructure facilities on their own. Small and medium scale units need quality infrastructure but may not have the means to pay for such facilities. For the SEZs to be viable, the user industries must be able to pay for the cost of the services provided. Only industries with a high value addition may be able to afford such high costs of developing infrastructural facilities.

SEZs should be targeted at small and medium scale industries with a focus on high value-added output. Pre-built factories provide readymade factory space which can cater to the needs of small and medium scale industries, serving as incubators before they grow in size and shift to a larger industrial space.

8.9 Global Experience

SEZs have been established in many countries as testing

grounds for implementation of liberal market economy principles. They are viewed as instruments to enhance the acceptability and credibility of transformation policies, to attract domestic and foreign investment, and generally for the opening up of the economy.

EPZs and SEZs were employed with considerable success by China and other ASEAN countries in the 1970s and 1980s to create regional islands, where export-oriented manufacturing could be undertaken. While EPZs in some of these countries had their share of early difficulties, they provided scope for cultivating manufacturing competitiveness when licensing, labour rigidities and high import duties and taxes acted as a disincentive for investment in the rest of the areas.

8.9.1 China: SEZs are called economic development areas (EDAs) in China. China set up four SEZs in the late 1970s on experimental basis to attract foreign capital, technology and managerial expertise. This was part of Chinese model of export-led growth. The astounding success of the SEZs in China has inspired other countries, including India to follow suit. Many in India believe that SEZs will create thousands of skilled and semi-skilled jobs in export-oriented industries and services and ensure double-digit growth rate in the future.

In China, the central government gives SEZs special policies and flexible measures, allowing SEZs to utilize a special economic management system.

1. Special tax incentives.
2. Greater independence on international trade activities.
3. Economic characteristics are represented as "4 principles":

- Construction primarily relies on attracting and utilising foreign capital.
- Primary economic forms are Sino-foreign joint ventures and partnerships as well as wholly foreign-owned enterprises.
- Products are primarily export-oriented.
- Economic activities are primarily driven by market.

SEZs are listed separately in the national planning

(including financial planning) and have province-level authority on economic administration. Following is the list of SEZs in China.

- Guangdong Province: Shenzhen, Zhuhai and Shantou.
- Fujian Province: Xiamen.
- Hainan Province (whole province).

8.9.2 North Korea: The Rajin-Sonbong Economic Special Zone was established under a UN economic development programme in 1994. Located on the bank of the Tumen River, the zone borders on the Yanbian Korean Autonomous Prefecture (or Yeonbyeon in Korean) of China, as well as Russia. In 2000, the name of the area was shortened to Rason and became separate from the North Hamgyeong Province.

8.9.3 Philippines: Philippine economic zones (eco-zones) are collections of industries, brought together geographically for the purpose of promoting economic development. Although designed to operate separately from the political and economic milieu of surrounding communities, Philippine economic zones do in fact interact with their neighbours. There are 41 private-owned economic zones and 4 government-owned economic zones in the Philippines. Of the 41 private economic zones, the biggest exporter is Gateway Business Park in General Trias, Cavite and the second biggest private eco-zone is Laguna Techno-park Inc. The four government-owned are Cavite Economic Zone, Bataan Economic Zone, Mactan Economic Zone and Baguio City Economic Zone.

9

Technology Parks

9.1 Importance of Science and Technology

The per capita income and quality of life that a nation enjoys is, in the final analysis, dependent largely on the technology it adopts, and which in turn has to be appropriate to its endowments, resources and skills.

The foundations of industrial and agricultural advance lie ultimately in the availability and effective use of human skills. Human skills are a formidable asset since they last not merely during one working life but because they are transmitted for generations. If these assets are used effectively, they may well turn out to be one of the most fruitful results of planning.

The pace of economic development depends on a variety of factors which constitute the psychological and sociological setting within which the economy operates. A major element in this setting is the community's will to progress and its readiness to develop and adopt new and more efficient methods and processes of production. Basically, development involves securing higher productivity all round and this is a function of the degree of technological advance the community is able to make. The problem is not one merely of adopting and applying the processes and techniques developed elsewhere, but of developing new techniques specially suited to local conditions.

Modern technology is changing rapidly and no country can hope to maintain a steady pace of advance unless it keeps abreast of current developments. Techniques in turn affect and are affected by economic and social organisation. Certain forms of economic and social organisation are unsuited to or incapable of absorbing new techniques and utilising them to the best advantage. To some extent techniques must of course be adapted to economic and social organisation, but the latter has also to change in order to accommodate new techniques which need to be applied not merely in one or two isolated lines but in several lines of economic activity.

The vital role of science in modern life is now generally recognised. Apart from the vast changes it has brought about, the development of a scientific temper in the people is considered important. Improvements in techniques evolved as a result of scientific research bring about great increases in production in the different sectors of the economy. National resources are augmented by the substitution of cheap and abundant materials for those in scarce supply and by finding uses for materials which have remained unutilised. A balanced programme of research covering every sector of the economy is essential therefore for the development of a country.

High standards of living in the more advanced countries are the direct result of progress in science and technology and the rapid pace of development associated with it. The flow of new scientific knowledge is continuous and ever expanding and covers both pure and applied research. Pure research leads to new knowledge and understanding of nature and its laws, and creates the scientific capital from which practical applications of knowledge are drawn. New products and processes are based on new principles and concepts. The advance of technology presents new problems to science and also provides new tools with which to resolve them.

9.2 Technology Park Defined

The ultimate objective of a technology park is to provide an environment that will enable the localization of various tech-related companies. It is a development that brings together office spaces, residential areas, and retail developments in order to enhance the operations of tech corporations, thereby providing various benefits and economies of scale to each individual business entity.

Technology parks are able to perfectly integrate row houses, residential complexes, villas, as well as low-rise and high-rise apartments with commercial and convenience establishments, clubs and resorts, and various facilities that make living and working as comfortable as possible. All of these amenities are ideally supposed to help in attracting investors and to promote the setting up of various businesses, ensuring that they get all they need to thrive and reach their operating objectives.

Usually, technology parks take some land space, and there is usually a lot of consideration given to them in order to thrive and wok towards their full potential.

9.3 Objectives of Technology Parks

However, the major purposes of technology parks are usually any of the following:

9.3.1 Advancement of Technology: The primary aim for the establishment of a technology park is usually the advancement of scientific and technological endeavours. Millions are usually poured into the creation of technology parks, and a large chunk of this money is spent on efforts such as research and development, experiments and other related efforts in the end, the goal is to come together and create an environment where science and technology are made to thrive and succeed.

9.3.2 Flow of Investment: It is a fact that technology is very profitable. In the event that a tech company is able to stand on its feet and gain enough popularity add recognition, there is no doubt to the fact that they will make enough money going forward. The prospect of being on the groundwork of something big is one of the major tools which the creators of technology parks use to attract investment, and its goal usually pays off the long-run. The investment received helps to develop the park, and also go into other aspects of human endeavour.

9.3.3 Establishment of Companies and Jobs Creation: Technology parks also create enabling environments for start-ups and tech companies to come and set up nicely. Companies are able to comfortably pursue their goals and work towards achieving set objectives. A direct consequence of company establishment, jobs are created, and more people are able to get suitable jobs.

9.3.4 Development of an Area: Due to the concentration of companies and the attraction of investment, infrastructural development in the general area, where the technology park is located, is definitely assured. This is why technology parks are usually founded in areas where the advancement of infrastructure might not necessary be the best. People living near the technology park are able to get jobs, and this will definitely be a relief to the overall economy of the country.

9.4 Software Technology Parks (STPs) in India

India has earned itself a reputation of an information technology (IT) superpower. STPs in India have played a seminal role in accomplishing this status. Today, STPs of India across over the country are synonymous with excellent infrastructure and statutory support aimed at furthering growth of IT in the country.

Software Technology Parks of India, is an autonomous society set up by the Ministry of Electronics and Information Technology (MeitY), Government of India in 1991, with the objective of encouraging, promoting and boosting the software exports from India.

Software Technology Parks of India maintains internal engineering resources to provide consulting, training and implementation services. Services cover network design, system integration, installation, operations and maintenance of application networks and facilities in varied areas.

9.4.1 Objectives of Software Technology Parks of India: These are as under:

1. To promote the development and export of software and software services including IT-enabled services/Bio-IT.
2. To provide statutory and other promotional services to the exporters by implementing schemes pertaining to software

technology parks and electronics and hardware technology parks and other such schemes which may be formulated by the Government from time-to-time.

3. To provide data communication services including value added services to IT/IT-enabled services related industries.
4. To promote micro, small and medium entrepreneurs by creating conducive environment for entrepreneurship in the field of IT/IT-enabled services.

10

Transport, Trade and Services

10.1 Transport Sector

An efficient transport system is a prerequisite for sustained economic development. It is not only the key infrastructural input for the growth process but also plays a significant role in promoting national integration, which is particularly important in a large country like India. In a liberalised set-up, an efficient transport network becomes all the more important in order to increase productivity and enhancing the competitive efficiency of the economy in the world market. The transport system also plays an important role of promoting the development of the backward regions and integrating them with the mainstream economy by opening them to trade and investment.

Worldwide, transport growth has been consistently higher than the economic growth due to specialisation, sourcing of material on a wider scale, the use of just-in-time strategies, increase and dispersal of retail and wholesale activities etc. The transport system in India has not been able to keep pace with these developments and considerable effort is required to correct the shortcomings.

Transport sector bears a close and complex relationship with all other sectors of the economy. While it tends to act as the prime mover of the development process, it must also respond to the development process, if the latter has to be smooth.

Transport plays a vital role in the economic development of the country. It must provide efficient and reliable transport services and it must accomplish these objectives at a minimum resource cost. The existing transport system comprises of several modes of transport amongst which rail and road transports predominate. Other modes of transport like shipping, pipelines, air transport are also important within their specialised areas considering the size of the country and its geographical features.

A more integrated approach is required to be taken of transport as a whole. The vision for transport should be guided by a modal mix that will lead to an efficient, sustainable, economical, safe, reliable, environmentally friendly and regionally balanced transportation system. Choices will need to be made on the priorities to be placed on different investments. Decisions on road expressways, dedicated rail freight corridors (DFCs), high speed trains and movement through inland waterways or coastal shipping must be taken holistically so that the objective of speed and efficient energy usage is achieved. Policy decisions should be based on life cycle energy costs of different transport modes.

It is necessary to foster the development of the various transport modes in an integrated manner that will lead to realization of an efficient, sustainable, safe and regionally balanced transportation system, where each mode of transport operates in its field of economy and usefulness, with competitive and non-discriminatory prices that are adequate to support progressive development of transport infrastructure and services. This would also enable the comparative advantages and economic efficiencies to be properly reflected in the user costs.

10.1.1 Railways: Railways are often referred to as the lifeline of an economy because of its predominance in transportation of bulk freight and long distance passenger traffic. Railways network criss-crosses the nation, binding it together by ferrying freight and passengers across the length and breadth of the country.

Railways are the principal mode of transportation for carrying bulk freight and long distance passenger traffic. Given India's continental size, geography, resource endowment and diversity, the railways play a key role in not only meeting the transport needs of the country, but also in binding together dispersed areas, thus, promoting national integration. It also plays a key role during war and emergencies when huge quantities of material and men are required to be moved across the country at a short notice.

Railways, without doubt, are among the main foundations on which the national economy rests. It provides a service which is safe, economical and efficient. In its operations, railways should always keep abreast of modem scientific and technological developments. Diesel and electric motive power, improved designs of wagons and coaches and improved signalling and telecommunication equipment have to be employed to an increasing extent in order to secure economy and efficiency. Improvements along these lines should lead to the operation of longer, heavier and, to the extent necessary, faster trains, thus securing fuller use of line capacity and rolling stock.

Upgrading technology in all spheres of activities needs greater attention so as to improve reliability, reduce maintenance cost and increase customer satisfaction. Technological improvements are needed in tracks, wagons, coaches, electric multiple units (EMUs) and locomotives. Tracks should be improved to cater to higher axle load and speed together with better methods to detect rail defects.

The rapid rise in international trade and domestic cargo has placed a great strain on tracks. The India government has, therefore, decided to build dedicated freight corridors in the high density routes. This will help to decongest these routes for freight movement and will increase the economic potential of the hinterland areas which will benefit from the reduced cost of transport. It will also provide spin off benefits in terms of location of industrial clusters along the new corridors attracting potential investment in a number of states.

The key challenge before any railway system it is not attracting additional traffic, but rather meeting the accelerating demand for high quality services imposed by a vibrant economy for which it has to take immediate and appropriate steps to augment capacity and deploy it optimally through new investment and tariff policies. Railways also has to execute projects speedily and procure assets at a rapid pace by incorporating best practices in project implementation, production and procurement of new assets.

Chinese railways is carrying 4.5 times more freight than Indian railways, mainly due to the larger investments made in Chinese railways in expanding and strengthening the infrastructure which also contributed towards improvements of productivity of Chinese railways. Indian railways carries more passengers than Chinese railways, but the long-term development of the railways in India depends crucially upon its ability to move freight, in keeping with the needs of the growing economy, and at speeds and reliability determined by the need to be competitive. This is especially important given the greater energy efficiency of the railways in the long distance freight.

To keep pace with the technological developments in various aspects of the railways sector, it is necessary to continuously upgrade the technology. Measures such as introducing longer trains and optimization of coach capacities have to be fully explored.

Speed differential between the freight and passenger trains has to be narrowed down by inducting high speed freight stock and upgrading freight terminals and their approaches, to obtain additional capacity in the medium term as well as to increase the reliability of service in freight business.

The application of information technology (IT) to various activities of railways also deserves special attention. IT applications hold the key to the railways sustained improvement in services and efficiency.

Railways, being the owners of vast tracts of land, can supplement its financial resources by certain non-tariff revenue measures like utilisation of land space for commercial purposes. In addition, the wide network of the railway's communication system can be leveraged to provide long distance (trunk) capacity for telecommunication purposes at much lower costs than would be entailed in laying new cables.

Railways remain an extremely important area, given the fact that transportation by rail has the highest energy efficiency as compared with other options. This suggests that if the institutional mechanisms come about, then the cost of transportation by railways would be much cheaper than that of transport by road. However, this is likely to require substantial reforms in the functioning of railways. The experience with the transformation of telecom, roads and ports serve as role models for the institutional change that may be required.

Development of capability in the railways is an urgent priority. Capacity in the Railways has lagged far behind what is needed and feasible, especially given the need to shift from road transport to rail in the interest of improving energy efficiency, and reducing the carbon footprint of development efforts. Expansion of the system must be accompanied by technological modernisation, greater attention to safety and steps to ensure financial viability.

10.1.2 Roads and Road Transport: Roads are the key to the development of an economy. A good road network constitutes the basic infrastructure that propels the development process through connectivity and opening up the backward regions to trade and investment. Roads also play a key role in inter-modal transport development, establishing links with airports, railway stations and ports. In addition, they have an important role in promoting national integration, which is particularly important in a large country like India.

Road transport has close linkages with the economic development and social integration of the country. It is the prime motorised mode of transport linking the remote and hilly areas with rest of the economy. The easy accessibility, flexibility of operation, door-to-door service and reliability have earned road transport an increasingly higher share of both passenger and freight traffic vis-à-vis other transport modes.

Substantial investment being made in the improvement of highways and an increase in the share of high value commodities in total freight would further boost the demand for road transport services.

A good road network is a critical infrastructure requirement for rapid growth. It provides connectivity to remote areas, provides accessibility to markets, schools, hospitals, opens up backward regions to trade and investment. Roads also play an important role in inter-modal transport development, establishing links with airports, railway stations and ports.

Road transport is considered to be one of the most cost effective and preferred mode of transport, both for freight and passengers, keeping in view its level of penetration into populated areas. Thus, it is vital to economic development and social integration of the country. Road transport has emerged as the dominant segment in India's transportation sector. Easy availability, adaptability to individual needs and cost savings are some of the factors which go in favour of road transport. Road transport also acts as a feeder service to railway, shipping and air traffic.

Public transport causes lesser environmental damage in terms of air and noise pollution, optimization of road space, increased per unit throughput and reduction in traffic congestion, as compared to personalized vehicles. Considering the advantage of public transport there is a need to strengthen the public transportation services through a policy regime, which fosters their financial viability and grants them more functional autonomy.

Roads are a service for all forms of development, whether of agriculture, trade, or industry. In the development of roads, a national conception is necessary not only because of their strategic importance but also because of the need for co-ordination between different types of roads.

Road transport is of great importance both for movement of passengers and goods. It is ideally suited for short and medium distances because of its inherent advantages such as easy availability and flexibility of operation, adaptability to individual needs, door to door service and reliability. It is also the main mechanised means of transport in hilly and rural areas not served by railways. Road transport provides one of the basic infrastructure facilities for economic development of backward areas besides being the feeder service to rail traffic, ports and harbours.

10.1.3 Shipping: Shipping is a critical infrastructure for the economic development of a country. It influences the pace, structure and pattern of development.

The maritime sector comprises of ports, overseas shipping, coastal shipping, inland water transport, shipbuilding and ship repair, ship breaking, maritime training, and international co-operation in maritime.

Ports perform multifarious activities. These include cargo handling, storage, warehousing, customs clearance, security and administration. Each of these activities can be considered as separate profit centres and appropriate policies should be evolved for commercialisation and private sector participation in each case. It may be better to make the ports work as corporate entities with administrative independence and the ability to raise finances for development.

A key insight in the area of ports has been the extent to which existing port facilities can yield better output given the better institutional mechanisms, without requiring substantial new investments. There are important experiments currently taking place across the country in terms of new contractual structures. They have already yielded results in terms of giving a sharp improvement as compared to the state of ports in India during the pre-reforms period. However, the performance of ports in India still lags far behind the standards seen in ports such as Singapore or Hong Kong. Looking forward, the key question that requires focus is establishment of a framework through which there is competition between multiple operators in a given port, and competition between ports.

Like many industries, the ship breaking industry has

grown and expanded in recent years all over the world. The ship breaking industry supplies substantial quantity of re-rollable and scrap steel for the iron and steel industry. It increases the availability of semi-finished material, which otherwise would have to be produced by using the ore. Thus, it helps in conservation of natural resources.

Ship breaking, as a regular commercial activity, started in some of the industrially advanced countries like the UK, US and Germany during the post-World War II period. By 1960, the activity shifted from the industrialized countries to other areas in Europe and Far East. However, more than 90 percent of ship breaking in the world in recent years has taken place in India, Bangladesh, Pakistan and China. Private entrepreneurs handle the task of ship breaking in India. It is a labour-intensive work and India, having abundant manpower, finds it a cost-efficient activity. Till the 1960s, ship breaking in India was confined mainly to dismantling of small barges and coastal wrecks. This activity grew into a full-fledged industry by 1979.

Ship breaking process is an industrial activity, which not only generates re-rollable steel but also helps create direct and indirect employment. Steel produced through the ship breaking route saves natural resources like iron ore, coal etc., which are used for production of steel through integrated steel plants. Re-rollable scrap produced by ship breaking saves one process of melting and thereby results in substantial saving in electrical energy consumption.

10.1.4 Civil Aviation: Air transport worldwide is the preferred mode of transport especially for long distance travel, business travel, accessing difficult terrains and for transporting high value and perishable commodities mainly on account of the speed of travel and saving of time. With the opening up of domestic skies to private carriers, air services have become affordable and are now effectively competing with other modes of transport.

The main advantage of civil aviation vis-à-vis railways and

road transport is the speed of travel and consequent saving of time. A part of this gain is, however, nullified for short-haul flights due to time taken in reporting, security checks, flying, luggage clearance etc. Air travel, nevertheless, retains a substantial edge over other modes of transport for long distance travel. It is particularly useful for business travel, international tourism and for transporting high value and perishable commodities. Air transport also provides easy accessibility to remote regions, which has implications for national integration and security. The advantage, however, has to be weighed against high cost of air travel and cost to the economy because of its high fuel intensity.

The civil aviation sector plays an important role in an economy. It provides fast and reliable mode of transport across the country and is particularly important for many areas/places still not adequately connected by rail or road. With increasing globalization, this sector will play a more significant role in integrating the Indian economy with the rest of the world.

It is now increasingly recognized that aviation, far from being a mere mode of transportation for a small elite group, makes an important contribution to the national economy and is crucial for sustainable development of trade and tourism. The civil aviation sector has made significant strides in coping with the growth of international and domestic traffic. This sector provides three categories of services, viz. operational, infrastructure and regulatory-cum-developmental.

The main objective of the development of the civil aviation sector is to provide world class infrastructure facilities and efficient, safe and reliable air services to meet the requirements of domestic and foreign trade and tourism. Meeting the air transport requirements of remote and inaccessible areas will also be a priority.

The increase in demand for air transport depends on a number of factors, which includes rate of growth of the economy and fall in real prices of air services. The airlines operate at very thin margins. The utilization of capacity becomes another important factor for determining the viability of air operators. In order that air transport plays its role in accordance with its comparative advantage, it is necessary to remove the bottlenecks affecting the sector. To enhance the operational efficiency in the civil aviation sector, the infrastructure facilities should be augmented, specifically to ensure full utilization of runways leading to improved payload. Other steps required include, extension of runways, use of satellite-based navigation system and allocation of optimal flights levels through a modern air traffic management system.

Air transport is a field for competitive development. The objective of development of air transport in the country, therefore, should be achieved through private sector participation on a much larger scale than before.

10.2 Trade and Commerce

International trade is an important element of world economy. Trade, internal and external, is as old as human civilization. Nations have been trading with each other since times immemorial. The importance of foreign trade differs from country to country. Normally, foreign trade is less important for countries having a wide geographical area and possessing a great variety of natural resources. Contrarily, the dependence on foreign trade is high for smaller countries endowed with less variety of resources.

10.2.1 Reasons for International Trade: Trade takes place because the facilities for the production of various goods are unequally distributed over the world. These facilities include: (a) mineral deposits (b) soil and climatic conditions, (c) labour skills etc. Based on these differences in factor endowments, different regions of the world and different regions within a country specialise in the production of goods for which they are best suited.

In fact, the basis for international trade is the same as for trade within a country, viz. geographical specialisation. In other words, both international trade and inter-regional trade have their root in territorial specialisation. As Swedish economist Bertil Ohlin observed, "International trade is but a special case of inter-local or inter-regional trade".

Why should then one study international trade separately? The study of international trade as a separate subject from inter-regional trade is necessitated because the former poses certain peculiar problems. These include the following:

1. Exchange rate determination because of different currencies involved in international transactions.
2. Balance of payments problem.
3. Barriers to international trade in the form of tariffs and quotas.

10.2.2 Theory of Absolute Advantage: It refers to a situation when out of two trading partner-countries, each one has an absolute cost advantage in producing a commodity (using similar and same quantities of resources) over the other. Suppose, there are two countries A and B both having only one factor of production (say labour) and producing two commodities X and Y. Country A produces 1 unit of commodity X with 5 units of labour and 1 unit of commodity Y with 3 units of labour while country B produces 1 unit of commodity X with 3 units of labour and 1 unit of Y with 4 units of labour. Then, it is said that country A has an absolute advantage in the production of commodity Y because 1 unit of its production requires 1 unit of labour less in it than in country B. Similarly, country B has an absolute advantage in the production of commodity X because 1 unit of it requires two units of labour less in it than in country A. This situation is considered to be the basis for territorial specialisation for the purpose of international trade. This view was propounded by Adam Smith (1723-1790) and later used by David Ricardo (1772-1823) in his theory of comparative cost.

10.2.3 Theory of Comparative Advantage: It is also known as theory of comparative cost. Propounded by British classical economist David Ricardo (1772-1823) to explain the basis for international trade, it states that trade takes place between two countries due to differences in the cost of production between them. One country may be more efficient than another in the production of every commodity (efficiency measured by factor inputs per unit of output); but it may be more efficient in the production of some commodities than others. According to Ricardo, a country should specialise in and export those commodities in which its comparative cost is less, i.e. comparative advantage is more. Alternatively, a country having disadvantage in the production of all commodities should specialise in and export that one in which its comparative disadvantage is less.

Suppose two countries A and B both produce machinery and textiles with the same production function employing only one factor of production, say labour. Country A uses 10 units of labour to produce a given machine and 6 units of labour to produce a given length of textile. Country B produces the same unit of machinery and textile with the help of 15 units and 7 units of labour respectively. Clearly, country B is producing both the goods at higher labour cost. It means country A is having absolute advantage in the production of both. Observing closely, we find that country A's comparative advantage is more in machinery where the cost ratio is 10:15 or 2:3 than in textiles where the ratio is 6:7 or 2:2.3.

According to this theory, country A should specialise in and export machinery where its comparative advantage is more while country B should specialise in and export textiles where its comparative disadvantage is less. Specialisation of this kind will bring both of them a bigger market and economies of scale leading to further reduction in the cost of production. Hence, both the countries will gain from trade.

10.2.4 Balance of Payments: Political and geographical boundaries of the world do not coincide with the natural resources, skills and other essentials for the betterment of human welfare. World trade and financial flows reflect sharp variances in needs and advantages among individual countries. At any given time some nations will show surpluses in trade and payment balances while others will experience corresponding deficits.

Balance of payments is a financial statement of a country showing the flows of goods, services and funds between its residents and those of rest of the world during a given period of time. It is based on double entry book-keeping system.

The process through which the authorities correct the balance of payments imbalance includes exchange rate variations, changes in government expenditure, checking imports/capital flows, inducing changes in economic structure and removing distortions and undesirable pressures.

10.2.5 Terms of Trade: By terms of trade we mean the rate at which a country's exports exchange against its imports. In other words, terms of trade indicate the relationship between the prices a country gets for its exports and the prices it pays for its imports. They are, thus, the ratio of export prices to import prices. They are expressed as follows:

$$t = \frac{Xp}{Mp}$$

where t = terms of trade, Xp = export price index and Mp = import price index.

If a country can influence export and import prices, it can improve terms of trade for itself. The power to influence export or import prices of a commodity depends upon the market share of a country. Sometimes, some countries may combine together—Organization of Petroleum Exporting Countries (OPEC)—and form a cartel for the purpose of importing and exporting a commodity. By such action they acquire a certain degree of monopoly power and are, therefore, able to influence world prices in their favour.

Terms of trade also depend on the elasticity of demand for a country's exports and imports. Higher the elasticity of demand for its exports, less advantageously it is placed in the world market. Higher the elasticity of demand for its imports, more favourably it is placed in the world market. In other words, terms of trade depend on reciprocal elasticity of demand of the two trading countries for each other's commodities. If India's demand for German machinery is relatively less elastic than German demand for Indian textiles, then India's terms of trade will be unfavourable in the sense that given demand conditions, machinery prices will rise more than those of textiles. For the given amount of machinery, India will have to export more quantity of textiles.

10.2.6 Exchange Rate: Exchange rate is the rate at which the currency of one country is converted into another currency. For example, ₹ 70 = 1 US$ is Indian rupee exchange rate for one US dollar. One of the most important conduits through which the world affects India's domestic well-being is the rupee (₹) exchange rate. The exchange rate is like a vital pipeline that links all of India to the rest of the world. It is through this that goods, services, and investments flow in and out of the country.

In the financial world, volatility in exchange rate adds to risks. Exchange rates can display higher volatility because of several factors such as deviation from fundamentals, excessive speculative activity, and macroeconomic shocks. Excessive fluctuations and volatility in exchange rates can spill over to other segments of financial markets, blur monetary policy signals and lead to financial stability problems. Excessive exchange rate fluctuations also have a detrimental impact on foreign trade and at times even on genuine investments. Investments can then be potentially guided by a view or a bet on exchange rate movements rather than by the underlying returns.

A. Purchasing Power Parity (PPP) Theory: Propounded by Gustav Cassel (1866-1944), this theory states that the rate of exchange of two currencies can be better determined by the price levels in the two countries, i.e. rate of exchange can be set where the purchasing power of the two currencies are equal to each other. Any change in exchange rate can also be explained in terms of changes in price levels from a given base level when the balance of payments was in adjustment. If prices in a country rise by 10 percent, the external value of the currency falls by 10 percent and vice versa.

PPP theory provided a point of reference for the long-run exchange rate in many of the modern exchange rate theories. Empirical evidence showed that PPP performs better for those countries that are geographically close to each other and where trade linkages are high. Moreover, PPP holds better for traded goods compared to non-traded goods. Reasons for failure of PPP may be attributed to the following:

1. Heterogeneity in the baskets of goods considered for construction of price indices in various countries,
2. Presence of transportation cost and other trade impediments like tariff,
3. Imperfect competition in goods market, and
4. Increase in the volume of global capital flows during the last few decades which led to sharp deviation from PPP.

10.3 Services Sector

There exists no precise definition of service. The term 'service' has been defined differently by different researchers and organizations at different points of time. In 1960, American Marketing Association (AMA) defined services as those "activities, benefits or satisfactions which are offered for sale, or provided in connection with the sale of goods". Though this definition was very popular at that time, one major problem with this definition was that it was not able distinguish between good and services.

A more precise definition of services can be as follows: A service is an activity or series of activities of more or less intangible nature that normally not necessarily, take place in interaction between the customer and service employees and/or physical resources and/or goods and/or system of the service provider which are provided as solution to customer problem. Banking and insurance services are cases in point.

10.3.1 Characteristics of Services: The marketing as well as services marketing literature recognize services as being different in nature from products. Services have four distinguishing characteristics, viz., intangibility, perishability, heterogeneity and inseparability, which differentiate them from goods. A brief discussion of these characteristics and their implications to services marketers is as follows:

A. Intangibility: The literature highlights intangibility as one of the key characteristics of services. Services are essentially intangible in nature and as such cannot be viewed or touched by the consumers. This has an important implication to the marketers in the sense that they cannot tell in advance to the customers as to what they will be getting. Unless the institutions supplying them have a good image and confidence among the customers, they may face difficulties in seeking customers' shares of mind and wallets. Service quality goes a long way in building favourable images in the minds of customers. The service marketers, therefore, have to focus on quality of their services to build their credibility and gain the trust of clients.

B. Inseparability: Services are referred to as being inseparable because services are delivered and consumed simultaneously and as such cannot be separated from the service provider. Since consumers are mostly present at the time of service delivery, they tend to affect or shape the performance and quality of service. Provision of good quality service, therefore, requires proper management of not only the employees, but also of customers so as to ensure that the interactions between the two are productive and capable of generating good quality service.

C. Heterogeneity: Services involve people, and people are all different. If not managed properly, service performance can differ not only from person to person, but also for a given person from day to day. There is, for instance, a strong possibility that the same enquiry would be answered slightly differently by different people (or even by the same person at different times). In other words, heterogeneity reflects the potential for high variability in service delivery and quality.

D. Perishability: In general, services cannot be stored and carried forward to a future time period. In simple words, perishability means inability to produce service in advance and store it for future use. For example, vacant seats on an airplane cannot be transferred to the next flight. In a similar vein, query-free times at the reference desk cannot be saved up until there is a busy period. Services are "time dependent" and "time important" which make them very perishable. Apart from requiring proper demand management, the perishabillity characteristic of services entails an important implication from the point of view of quality management. This is so because while goods can be produced in advance and inventoried for future sale, this is not possible with services. Services in general are produced and delivered simultaneously or immediately as and when demanded by the customers, and these are as such not amenable to pre-delivery quality controls as is the case with the goods.

These characteristics of services make evaluation and purchase of services a difficult task for the consumers.

Part III
Environmental Geography

11

Environment and Development: Conflict and Balance

11.1 What is Environmental Geography?

Environmental geography is the branch of geography that describes the spatial aspects of interactions between humans and the natural world. It is the study of systematic description of different components of environment and interactions of man with these components.

Environmental geography is the study of characteristic features of various components of the environment, the interactions between and among the components in a geo-ecosystem in terms of ecosystem of varying spatial and temporal scales.

Productivity of an economic system depends, to a large extent, on the supply and quality of its natural resources. In fact, natural and environmental resources are the basis of all economic activities. Soil, forests, mines, water, air and other natural resources are productive assets of an economy. Poor quality of water and air adversely affects the health of population, causing reduced labour productivity and premature mortality. Similarly, soil degradation and erosion leads to reduced and inferior quality of agricultural output.

11.2 Environment and Development: The Conflict

Economic development often depends on the utilisation and conversion of natural resources into useful goods and services. This process of consumption and conversion uses energy, minerals and other natural resources such as air, water, land and bio-diversity. It also produces wastes which are released into environment with adverse impacts.

Economic activities, in turn, affect the quantity and quality of natural and environmental resources. Mining, lumbering, manufacturing, fishing and a host of other economic activities change the stock of natural resources which calls for appropriate trade-off between the needs of present and future generations.

Increase in economic activities—due to growing population and/or enhanced consumption levels—often impacts environment negatively. Degradation of natural resources and losses in environmental quality adversely affect people at large. As a consequence of high level of economic activities, emissions, effluents and waste discharges exceed the carrying capacity of different resources. Economic growth without environmental considerations can cause serious damage to the quality of life of the present and future generations. It is in this context that economists distinguish between economic growth and economic development. Economic growth means sustained increase in per capita real income. Economic development is a much wider term. It includes economic growth and at the same time encompasses questions regarding patterns of production, distribution of national income, consumption behaviour of the people and concern for environment.

Economic progress improves our standard of living and makes our life more comfortable. On the other hand, it is this very progress that can lead to degradation of the environment. Any increase in national income would arise only from increased production of goods and services involving greater consumption of resources such as land, forest, fuels etc. whose supply is, essentially, limited. While some of these resources may be renewable, others get depleted and, ultimately, exhausted with continuous use. Any attempt to preserve the non-renewable resources might require compromising on the growth rates.

Conflict between economic development and environment is, essentially, a conflict between short- and long-run priorities, between the interests of current and future generations. Large exploitation of natural resources today, while increasing the economic growth for the current generations, would lead to gradual exhaustion and degradation of these resources, thereby reducing their availability to our future generations and adversely affecting their output, income and living standards.

11.2.1 Environmental Pollution: Demographic expansion, over exploitation of natural resources, mega development projects—with least concern for sustainability and conservation—have greatly affected the environment. The magnitude and alterations that humanity can make to environment, threaten to undermine the basic natural process that sustains biosphere. The process of economic development necessarily entails exploitations of natural resources. However, when such exploitation becomes indiscriminate and is undertaken without adequate environmental safeguards, the consequences can be disastrous.

Pollution can be defined as an undesirable change in the physical, chemical, or biological characteristics of the air, water or land that can harmfully affect health, survival or activities of human beings or other living organisms. Pollution refers essentially to a process by which a resource is rendered unfit for some beneficial use. Of the various kinds of pollution (air, water, land, noise, radiation and odour) that affect the quality of life in India, water pollution is by far the most serious in its implications for the health and well-being of the people.

Environmental pollution is one of the major problems faced by the world community, especially in the cities of the developing countries which have experienced unbridled growth of population, urbanization and industrialization. Municipal services—such as water supply and sanitation, drainage of storm water, management of solid and hazardous wastes, supply of adequate and safe food and housing—are unable to keep pace with urban growth. The unplanned location of industries in and around urban areas and volume of traffic have caused serious pollution problems. All these factors have led to deteriorating environmental conditions, adversely impacting the health of the people.

Pollution has become a major threat to the very existence of mankind on this earth. Pollution of various resources has gone to such an extent that people are unable to breathe fresh air and drink fresh water. True, advancements in science and technology have added to human comforts by way of automobiles, electrical appliances, supersonic jets, modern medicines, communications and entertainment. However, these blessings have been diluted by serious problems posed by ecological imbalances and climate changes.

Environmental degradation not only affects us but also has repercussions for future generations. Globally, the need for sustainable development is being emphasized. Sustainable development attempts to strike a balance between the demands of economic development and the need for protection of our natural environment.

11.3 Sustainable Development: The Balancing Act

The concept of sustainable development is inextricably linked with environment protection. It is a strategy for improving the quality of human life while living within the carrying capacity of supporting eco system. It is clear from the above definition that sustainable development entails commitment, protection and preservation.

Sustainable development is that which meets the needs of the present without compromising the ability of future generations. The heaviest burden in international economic adjustment has been carried by the world's poorest population. The consequence has been the considerable increase in human distress and over exploitation of land and water resources to ensure survival in the short term. Further, the desire to solve all social and human problems at one stroke has influenced the pace of development. Its reaction is visible in the atmosphere and in natural, physical and social environment. Awareness regarding the consequences of this event has developed into a consensus referred to as ecological concern.

Sustainable development advocates economic progress in an environmentally responsible manner. Sustainable development attempts to strike a balance between the requirements of economic development and the need for protection of the environment. It seeks to combine the elements of economic efficiency, inter-generational equity, social concerns and environmental protection. Although, the term sustainable development has many interpretations, it generally refers to non-declining human well-being over time.

Economic growth and development have to be guided by the compulsion of sustainability, because no country can afford to ignore the economic as well as the environmental threat that a fast-deteriorating ecosystem poses to its economy. No country is immune to the reality of climate change, ecological degradation, depletion of the ozone layer and contamination of freshwater.

Sustainable development is a difficult balancing act in countries with low incomes. Society has to simultaneously accomplish three things with trade-offs: improve economic well-being with social justice for the present generation, yet manage with more restrained use of land, air, forest, energy, and water resources, and protect future generations. The choices are more difficult in developing countries because they affect people's livelihoods. Such a 'stewardship' to succeed therefore needs to respond to people's needs, share information on choices and costs, and ensure participation and ownership.

11.3.1 Environmental Economics: It is a branch of economics which deals with the inter-relationships between environment and development. Environmental economics examines the interface between economic agents and environment. Economic activities of human beings have a profound impact on natural environment. Hence, use/abuse of natural resources has raised many moral, legal and practical questions for present and future generations. There has been a gradual shift in many developed countries from command and control type of policy approach to environmental policy goals. Presently, many governments require cost-benefit analysis of policy options with regard to changes in environmental legislations by resetting environmental standards and introducing new policy instruments for environmental protection. Environmental economics has also made significant contributions to valuation techniques and design of new policy instruments for pollution control and management.

It is often said that gross domestic product (GDP) is not the best way of measuring the true well-being of nations, because the pursuit of growth can be at the cost of the environment. Conventional ways of measuring GDP in terms of production do not take into account the environmental damage caused by production of goods and services. Only after GDP is adjusted for environmental costs, the growth of adjusted GDP can be called a measure of the increase in total production in the economy. There is obviously a two-way relationship between environment and economic growth. Natural resources and raw materials such as water, timber and minerals directly provide inputs for the production of goods and services.

11.3.2 Environmental Management: Due to its cross-cutting nature, and wide local and global stakeholder base, environmental governance needs to be strategic. An ideal framework should be anticipative, technically oriented, cognizant of legal issues, geo-politically relevant and forward-looking, capable of maximising national interests and progressive enough to make a social impact. Most importantly, management of the environment should include progressively adapting/changing actions that rely on sound scientific, technological, human-cognitive and collaborative principles.

11.3.3 Green Growth: Green growth involves rethinking growth strategies with regard to their impact on environmental sustainability and the environmental resources available to poor and vulnerable groups. It is significant to note that many stimulus packages announced globally to combat recession incorporated a green component. International experience is that green growth promotes inclusivity. Further, the renewable energy sector is relatively labour-intensive, with the potential for generating more jobs than the oil and gas industries.

Environment must not be considered as just another sector of national development. It should form a crucial guiding dimension for plans and programmes in each sector. This becomes clear only if the concern for environmental protection is understood in its proper context. Ecological degradation compromises the quality of life in the long-run.

A. Requirements of Green Growth: Low-carbon green growth is a pattern of development that decouples economic growth from carbon emissions, pollution and resource use, and promotes growth through the creation of new environment-friendly products, industries and business models that also improve people's quality of life. Thus, low-carbon green growth entails the following:

1. Using less energy, improving the efficiency with which resources are used and moving to low-carbon energy sources.
2. Protecting and promoting the sustainable use of natural resources such as forests and peat lands.
3. Designing and disseminating low-carbon technologies and business models to reinvigorate local economies.
4. Implementing policies and incentives which discourage carbon intensive practices.

Green growth is not anti-growth. Rather, it represents a change in how we manage economies to reflect a broader conception of what constitutes effective and sustainable growth. Environmental assets—water, land, air, ecosystems and the services they provide—represent a significant share of a country's wealth. Just like physical and human capital, natural capital requires investment, maintenance, and good management if it is to be productive and fully contribute to prosperity.

Green growth requires policies that are on their own terms

good for growth, as well as for the environment, such as reforming energy subsidies or trade barriers that protect pollution-intensive sectors. It entails politically difficult reforms in the patterns of pricing, regulation, and public investment, and it calls for complex changes in behaviours and social norms. Importantly, green growth requires knowing when to go for the politically expedient rather than the economically optimal.

B. Advantages of Green Growth: The amount of CO_2 a country emits into the atmosphere depends on a wide range of factors, including the size of its economy, the level of industrialization, and the efficiency of its energy use, as well as population, lifestyle choices and land use changes. As a consequence of rapid and carbon-intensive growth, the Asian region has been fast becoming a major source of greenhouse gas emissions. The transition to a low-carbon economy will benefit emerging Asia in the following ways:

1. Many low-carbon interventions have important co-benefits for Asia at different levels, including the enhanced energy security associated with energy efficiency (on both the supply and demand side) and renewable energy projects. Human health benefits from interventions that reduce air pollutants, such as those from transport; and the environmental benefits that can be achieved through forestry and agricultural management, waste reduction programmes and employment programmes.
2. Interventions, which have positive economic rates of return and short pay-back time and should be undertaken irrespective of climate change considerations, can contribute substantially to the economic development of emerging Asian countries.
3. Asian countries that pursue low-carbon development, including the transfer of financial resources through the carbon market and new public programmes that support the reduction of emissions are likely to reap strategic and competitive advantage at the regional and international levels.

4. Emerging countries of Asia are likely to suffer disproportionately from the impacts of climate change (drought, increased severity of tropical storms, sea level rise, etc.). Asia has a strong interest in becoming a leading participant in global efforts on both emissions reduction and adaptation.
5. Low-carbon green growth will become more important as countries seek to take a pro-poor, pro-employment economic development path based on innovation.
6. Emerging Asia will have real social gains in the low-carbon green growth process by involving local communities to promote equity and fairness, along with improved air quality and other eco-system services.
7. Emerging Asia will become a leader in key green technologies and business models, and an important destination for the commercialization of key low-carbon technologies, green products and services.
8. Emerging Asia will be able to sweep away the short-term developmental thinking that has plagued the past several decades and replace it with paths delivering development that flourishes within ecological limits.

Low-carbon green growth is a unique opportunity to invest in change. Many analysts believe that the sooner emerging Asian countries take advantage of low-carbon green growth, the better it will be for their long-term development prospects, economic restructuring and their quest to find new drivers of growth. Even though the transition to a low-carbon green growth paradigm is a long-term process, the following years are crucial for Asia to seize the economic, social and environmental opportunities, gain competitive advantage and show global leadership through regional cooperation.

11.3.4 Inclusive Green Growth: Sustainable development has three pillars: economic, environmental, and social sustainability. We cannot presume that green growth is inherently inclusive. Green growth policies must be carefully designed to maximize benefits for, and minimize costs to, the poor and most vulnerable, and policies and actions with irreversible negative impacts must be avoided.

Rapid growth is necessary to meet the urgent development needs of the world's poor. However, growth will be unsustainable in the long-run unless it is both socially inclusive and green—the latter by ensuring that the earth's natural assets are able to adequately provide the resources and environmental services on which humans depend. Inclusive green growth requires tackling political economy constraints, overcoming deeply entrenched behaviours and social norms, and developing innovative financing instruments to change incentives and promote innovation, and thus address the market, policy, and institutional failures that lead to the overuse of natural assets. Greener growth is necessary, efficient, and affordable. It should focus on what needs to happen in the next 20 to 30 years to avoid getting locked into unsustainable paths and causing irreversible environmental damage.

Economic and social sustainability, on the one hand, and social and environmental sustainability, on the other, have been found to be not only compatible, but also largely complementary. Not so with economic and environmental sustainability, as growth has come largely at the expense of the environment which is why green growth aims to ensure that economic and environmental sustainability are compatible.

12

Biodiversity and Ecosystems

Biodiversity and ecosystem services are freely available public goods and all of humankind, particularly the poor, depends on them for their livelihood.

12.1 Range of Biodiversity

Biodiversity is the variability among living organisms and ecological complexes of which they are part, including diversity within and between species and ecosystems. Biodiversity has direct consumptive value in food, agriculture, medicine and industry.

Human activities—both directly and indirectly—responsible for presently high rates of biodiversity and habitat loss include the following:

1. Fragmentation and degradation due to agricultural activities.
2. Extraction activities including mining, fishing, logging and harvesting.
3. Human settlements, industry and associated infrastructure.

Habitat loss and fragmentation leads to the formation of isolated, small and scattered populations.

Strategies and actions required to protect bio-wealth should include the following:

1. Formulation of conservation and prudent use strategies for each significant catalogued wetland, with participation from local communities, and other relevant stakeholders.
2. Formulation and implementation of eco-tourism strategies for identified wetlands through multi-stakeholder partnerships involving public agencies, local communities, and investors.
3. Integration of wetland conservation (including conservation

of village ponds and tanks) into sectoral development plans for poverty alleviation and livelihood improvement, and linking efforts for conservation and sustainable use of wetlands with the ongoing rural infrastructure development and employment generation programmes.

12.2 Ecosystems

India has an unparalleled range of natural ecosystems because of its wide latitudinal range, varied physiognomic features, diverse climatic regimes, long coastlines and tropical islands. Human societies—with a long-standing conservation ethos anchored in the cultural and religious traditions of several millennia—have used this natural bounty. This use has gradually given rise to rich secondary ecosystems, which have their own unique assemblages of floral and faunal communities and are the notable abodes of large agglomerations of spectacular animals and birds.

Water and fertile soil are the two most important pre-requisites of India's food security. Both are irrevocably linked with forest and watershed conservation. The gravity and consequences of India's water scarcity are as yet not fully realized and hence it has not yet been universally acknowledged that the greatest product of forests—both qualitative as well as quantitative—is water. Natural vegetation, both forests and grasslands, are the prime conservers of soil and the providers of nutrients and humus. The functional lifespan of most of hydro-projects has been drastically reduced due to exponential siltation, caused by overuse and abuse of forests and rangelands.

Grasslands are the only breeding grounds of a number of avian species, whose nesting time is the monsoon. Due to the presence of crops in the fields, the monsoon is the period most affected by free-ranging livestock, who have nowhere else to go. This is the time when the grass grows. If grass is over-grazed at this time, it not only prevents fodder production and seed formation, but nests of ground-living birds are also trampled. No grasslands, however resilient, can bear the overuse and abuse that they are subjected to presently.

12.3 Biosphere Reserves

The programme of Biosphere Reserve was initiated under the Man and Biosphere (MAB) programme by UNESCO in 1971. The purpose of the formation of the biosphere reserve is to conserve *in situ* all forms of life, along with its support system, in its totality, so that it could serve as a referral system for monitoring and evaluating changes in natural ecosystems. In the current situation, the selection of a biosphere reserve is based on considerations, which are generally ad hoc. In all instances, significant areas of biosphere reserves are managed either as sanctuaries or national parks and as such all the applicable restrictions in such PAs are operative.

Biosphere Reserves are areas of terrestrial and coastal ecosystems which are internationally recognized within the framework of UNESCO's Man and Biosphere (MAB) programme. These Reserves are required to meet a minimal set of criteria and adhere to a minimal set of conditions before being admitted to the World Network of Biosphere Reserves designated by UNESCO. The world's major ecosystem types and landscapes are represented in this network, which is devoted to conserving biological diversity, promoting research and providing models of sustainable development in the service of human kind with special reference to the local communities which mostly consist of traditional societies.

These Reserves are rich in biological and cultural diversity and encompass unique features of exceptionally pristine nature. The goal is to facilitate conservation of representative landscapes and their immense biological diversity and cultural heritage, foster economic and human development which is culturally and ecologically sustainable and to provide support for research, monitoring, education and information exchange.

There is a compelling conservation need to set aside sufficient representative examples of biotic provinces to extend protection to entire community of species in viable terrestrial and marine ecosystems to be designed as *biosphere reserves*. The concept of such Reserves was evolved under UNESCO's Man and Biosphere (MAB) Programme with the following objectives:

1. To save for the present and future human use the diversity and integrity of biotic communities of plants and animals within natural ecosystems, and to safeguard the genetic diversity of species on which their continuing evolution depends.
2. To provide areas for ecological and environmental research, including baseline studies, both within and adjacent to those reserves.
3. To provide facilities for education and training.

The biosphere reserves should comprise not only completely natural ecosystems but also semi-natural established land-use practices. Among such reserves, areas that have outstanding potential for restoration to natural conditions, should also be included. Biosphere reserves are not meant to substitute established national parks and sanctuaries but may often coincide partly with national parks and sanctuaries.

There is a need to develop guidelines for the formation of biosphere reserves, which lay down clearly not only the criteria but also the management implications. In the existing situation, it is not clear as to how the object of a biosphere reserve is significantly different from national parks and sanctuaries.

12.4 Convention on Biological Diversity (CBD)

Convention on Biological Diversity (CBD)—one of the key agreements adopted during the Earth Summit held in Rio de Janeiro in 1992—is the first comprehensive global agreement which addresses all aspects relating to biodiversity. The CBD, which has near universal membership with 192 countries as its Parties, sets out commitments for maintaining the world's ecological underpinnings, while pursuing economic development.

The Convention, while reaffirming sovereign rights of

nations over their biological resources, establishes 3 main goals: (a) conservation of biological diversity, (b) sustainable use of its components and (c) fair and equitable sharing of the benefits arising out of the use of genetic resources. India is a party to the CBD.

India has been responding to various notifications being received from the CBD Secretariat, *inter alia*, by making submissions, and nominating experts for various expert group meetings. India has prepared its Fourth National Report through a consultative process and submitted it to the CBD Secretariat.

12.5 Biological Diversity Act, 2002

In pursuance to the CBD, India enacted the Biological Diversity Act in 2002 following a widespread consultative process. The Biological Rules were notified thereafter in 2004. The Act gives effect to the provisions of the CBD. It also addresses access to biological resources and associated traditional knowledge to ensure equitable sharing of benefits arising out of their use to the country and its people, thereby contributing to achieving the third objective of the CBD. India is one of the first few countries to have enacted such legislation. The Act is implemented through a three-tiered institutional structure: National Biodiversity Authority (NBA), State Biodiversity Boards (SBBs) and Biodiversity Management Committees (BMCs).

With effect from October 1, 2003, National Biodiversity Authority (NBA), Chennai, is a body corporate established in accordance with the provisions of Section 8 of the Biological Diversity Act, 2002.

NBA has so far supported creation of State Biodiversity Boards (SBBs) in 29 States and has also facilitated establishment of 37,769 biodiversity management committees (BMCs).

12.6 Convention on International Trade in Endangered Species of Wild Fauna and Flora (CITES)

In order to regulate international trade in endangered

species of wildlife, CITES (also known as Washington Convention) was signed in March 1973. The Government of India signed the Convention in July 1976, which was ratified in October 1976. The Director, Wildlife Preservation has been designated as the CITES Management Authority for India. India was also represented in the Animal Committee meeting of CITES held in Geneva in April 2009.

CITES is a very important treaty for the conservation of species. As on October 20, 2016, 183 countries were signatories to it. CITES—through its once-in-two year Conference of Parties and intervening Committee Meetings—decides on the protection levels that need to be accorded to various species in international trade, by placing them in different Appendices. For example, species in Appendix I are banned from international trade, those in Appendix II have a certain regulatory regimen on trade and those in Appendix III have regulations applicable only to those species and derivatives that come from a certain region. India has been an active member at all meetings of CITES, particularly in the area of tiger, elephant and Tibetan antelope conservation.

A resolution on the conservation of Asian Cats was proposed by India in November 2002, during the XII meeting of the Conference of Parties to the CITES. This resolution was adopted. Whale shark is a highly endangered species. India, Philippines and Madagascar sponsored a joint proposal for inclusion of whale shark in Appendix II of CITES, which was ratified at the Conference of Parties in Santiago, Chile. Also, India and US jointly sponsored a proposal for including all species of roofed turtles of genus Kachuga, in Appendix II, which was also ratified in the XII meeting of the Conference of Parties to the CITES.

12.7 World Heritage Convention (WHC)

WHC is responsible for listing of world heritage sites, which include both cultural and natural sites. WHC is a Convention under the aegis of the United Nations Educational, Scientific and Cultural Organization (UNESCO). India is a member of WHC and the Wildlife Wing of the Ministry of Environment, Forest and Climate Change (MoEFCC) is associated with conservation of the natural world heritage sites.

Presently, 5 natural world heritage sites in India have been recognized by UNESCO, viz:

1. National Park, Kaziranga.
2. National Park, Manas.
3. National Park, Keoladeo.
4. Nanda Devi National Park.
5. Sundarbans National Park.

Apart from these, the Valley of Flowers National Park has also been included in the list of world heritage sites as an extension to Nanda Devi National Park. 4 new natural heritage sites—Western Ghats cluster, Kangchendzonga National Park, Namdhapha National Park and Wild Ass Sanctuary, Little Rann of Kutch—have been included in the tentative list of world heritage sites.

India participated in the 33rd Session of the World Heritage Committee that was held in Seville, Spain from June 22 to 30, 2009. The Committee encouraged India to prepare the tentative list of its outstanding natural sites and submit details for future nominations. Recognition as world heritage site helps in: (a) improving conservation values and status, (b) socio-economic development through enhanced funding support, (c) increasing eco-tourism activity and conservation awareness among the masses and (d) enhances the significance of the site in the eyes of the people and the government.

12.8 Marine Biodiversity

12.8.1 Marine Ecosystems: There is inadequate knowledge and understanding of the country's valuable marine ecosystems, and total absence of protective measures against wanton exploitation and destruction of these resources.

The coral reefs, rich in limestone, have been thoughtlessly plundered for the manufacture of cement in the Gulf of Mannar (Tamil Nadu) and in the Pirotan Islands (Gujarat), thus exposing the coastal areas to sea erosion. These rare and unique ecosystems need urgent protection as *marine reserves*.

Similarly, India's coastal mangroves constitute rich ecosystems which contain many unique species adapted to the unusual habitat and are also key nursery areas for many species of fish which need protection. These mangroves, which form a vital protection against cyclone damage, have already been lost from most of coastal areas, and now deserve full protection where they still exist.

Some of the Island ecosystems of the Andaman and Nicobar and Lakshdweep groups are very rich and delicately balanced but vulnerable to intrusions. These islands need to be scientifically surveyed and protected in appropriate reserves under technical management.

12.8.2 National Institute of Coastal and Marine Biodiversity, Kanyakumari: Marine biodiversity has immense potential for contributing to the economy of India as a large part of India's population subsists on the resources available to them along the country's long coastal region, in 53 coastal districts of 10 maritime States and 6 Union Territories including the Andaman and Nicobar and Lakshadweep. Marine biodiversity forms the main employment as well as material generating resource. However, the scientific aspects of the management of marine biodiversity have not received the attention it deserves.

The Ministry of Environment, Forest and Climate Change (MoEFCC) has initiated the process of establishment of a National Institute for Coastal and Marine Biodiversity. The Wildlife Institute of India, Dehradun, has been entrusted with the task for development of the Institute.

12.8.3 Olive Ridley Turtle Conservation Project: A significant proportion of the world's Olive Ridley turtle population nests at nesting sites along the eastern coast of India. This endangered species of sea turtles is also a focus of attention of the international community which looks up to India to provide safety to the nesting sites and to the turtle populations that seasonally arrive there for the propagation of their species. The Sea Turtle Conservation Project initiated by the Ministry of Environment and Forest (MoEF), in collaboration with UNDP in November 1999, has been completed and the report published by the Wildlife Institute of India (WII).

The Project has identified and made an inventory map of the breeding sites of sea turtles, developed guidelines to safeguard the species and minimize turtle mortality caused by human activities. It has also prepared tourism guidelines for ecotourism in sea turtle areas and has developed national and international co-operative and collaborative plans of action for sea turtle conservation. A significant achievement of the project has been the use of satellite telemetry to trace the migratory route of Olive Ridley turtles in the seas, and the sensitization of fishermen and the State Government of Orissa to the use of the turtle excluder device (TED) by the fishing trawlers, to check turtle mortality in fishing nets.

12.8.4 International Whaling Commission (IWC): IWC was set up under the International Convention for the Regulation of Whaling which was signed in Washington on December 2, 1946. The purpose of the Convention is to provide for conservation of whale stocks. India has been a member of the International Whaling Commission since 1981 and has played a pro-active and prominent role in bringing about a moratorium on commercial whaling and supporting the Commission in its efforts towards whale conservation. The 61st Annual meeting of the Commission was held in Madeira, Portugal from June 22 to 26, 2009 with representation from India.

12.8.5 Coral Reefs: 4 major coral reef areas identified for intensive conservation and management are: (a) Gulf of Mannar, (b) Gulf of Kachchh, (c) Lakshadweep and (d) Andaman and Nicobar Islands. The emphasis is on preventive aspects through monitoring and surveillance as the restoration work is both costly and time consuming. MoEF provides financial assistance to the State Forest Departments of all the 4 identified coral reef areas in the country for activities like monitoring, surveillance, education and awareness. Besides, MoEF also supports R&D activities with emphasis on targeted research on coral biodiversity, its management including various aspects of pollution in these areas.

The Indian reef area is estimated to be 2,375 square kilometres. For encouraging targeted research on both hard and soft corals in the country, MoEFCC has established a National Coral Reef Research Centre in Port Blair.

12.8.6 Coastal Zone Management: Coastal areas are currently classified in four categories (CZ 1 to 4) with different principles for development activities. Category 1 includes ecologically sensitive areas, category 4 includes islands and categories 2 and 3 permit construction activities based on vulnerability. The Swaminathan Committee prescribed that the local circumstances and vulnerabilities should be the basis of coastal zone management and regulations. For this purpose, use of scientific, social, and local information should be made in environmental management plans for coastal areas. Conservation of life forms (and their habitats such as nesting/spawning sites) and integration of their environments with human well-being should be essential components of such plans. Participation of civil society and fishing/coastal communities in the State level coastal zone management committees should be ensured for conservation and sustainable harvests.

Inland aquatic systems cover 5.3 percent of India's land area but harbour 15 percent and 20 percent of India's floral and faunal diversities respectively. There are wide gaps in knowledge relating to hydrological parameters, ecosystem processes and aquatic life forms in these systems. Information on physico-chemical aspects of water quality in rivers and lakes has become available largely because of the support from Central Pollution Control Board (CPCB), but that on aspects such as area, depth, hydrology and ecosystem processes (functions) is practically non-existent. The existing programmes on conservation accordingly need a revamp.

12.8.7 Siberian Crane Conservation Project: The

Working Group on Environment and Natural Resources is an important component of the Indo-Russian Inter-governmental Commission. In its meeting held in April 2003 in Moscow, several important decisions were taken which included the Siberian Crane Conservation Project for introduction of captive-bred Siberian crane chicks in the flock of common cranes, so that the migration of the Siberian cranes to India can be revived and the loss of this magnificent bird to India in recent years regained.

13

Global Climate Change

Climate change is a serious global environmental concern, which is primarily caused by the building up of greenhouse gases in the atmosphere. Recent discourse on climate change has underscored the fact that climate change occupies a high priority on the environmental agenda of international community.

Global climate change due to rising levels of green house gases (GHGs) in the atmosphere is one of the most serious environmental concerns of present time. The accumulated scientific evidence clearly indicates that if the rate of GHG emissions is not reduced very significantly, there will be a damaging effect on the global climate.

Since global warming is caused by total accumulation of GHG and each country's emissions add to the stock, the cost of each country's emissions is borne by the entire global community. Similarly, the benefits of reduction in emission by any one country accrue not to the country itself but to the entire global community. This is classically a situation characterized by externalities in which individual countries will not have a sufficient incentive to undertake mitigation unless all countries co-operate in what is felt to be a collective effort with an equitable distribution of the burden of reducing emissions.

13.1 Evidence on Climate Change

The Intergovernmental Panel on Climate Change (IPCC), established in 1988 by the World Meteorological Organization (WMO) and the United Nations Environment Programme (UNEP), has worked extensively on evaluating past trends and the future prospects of climate change. IPCC reviews and assesses the most recent scientific, technical, and socio-economic information produced worldwide relevant to climate change.

According to IPCC, the global temperature may rise by 2-4.5 degree centigrade by the end of this century, including a 2.7-4.3°C increase over India by 2080s if adequate actions are not taken to reduce emissions globally. At the national level, the observed increase in surface air temperatures over the past century is 0.4 degree centigrade.

13.1.1 The Fourth Assessment Report (AR4) of IPCC, 2007: AR4 of IPCC, released in November 2007, concluded that the fact of global warming is unequivocal and there is enough evidence to indicate that this is due to anthropogenic reasons. Recent years have been the warmest since 1860, the year from when regular instrumental records are available. It is important to note that global warming will affect mankind seriously.

AR4 of IPCC brought climate change issue to the fore and led the parties to make serious efforts to address the problem through long-term cooperative actions as agreed under the Bali Action Plan. [1] IPCC made serious projections of the future scenario in terms of global warming and predicted that there may be adverse impact of climate change on agriculture, water resources, eco-systems, sea levels, human health and result in rise in extreme weather events.

13.1.2 Fifth Assessment Report (AR5) of IPCC, 2014: IPCC in its AR5 observed that there has been an increasing trend in the anthropogenic emissions of greenhouse gases (GHGs) since the advent of the industrial revolution, with about half of the anthropogenic CO_2 emissions during this period occurring in the last 40 years. The period 1983-2012 is likely to have been the warmest 30 year period of the last 1,400 years. CO_2 emissions from fossil fuel combustion and industrial processes have contributed a major portion of total GHG emissions during the period 1970-2010.

The change in the climate system is likely to have adverse impact on the economy, livelihoods, cropping pattern, and food security. According to the various projections by the IPCC, extreme heat events are likely to be longer and more intense in addition to changes in precipitation patterns. The change in climate could: (a) affect the production of wheat, rice, and maize in the tropical and temperate zones, (b) have negative impact on health by exacerbating health problems that already exist especially in developing countries and (c) adversely impact productive activities like growing food and working outdoors.

The ecological overshoot problem, i.e. the ecological footprint being larger than the bio-capacity of the population, is an important issue in the global climate discourse. The *overshoot* can also be understood in terms of the carbon budget. The risk of climate change is largely a function of total cumulative GHGs in the atmosphere. IPCC AR5 has estimated that for temperature increase to remain below 2°C of pre-industrial levels the world can emit only about 2,900 Giga tonnes (Gt) of CO_2 from all sources from the industrial revolution till 2100. Till 2011, the world has emitted 1,900 Gt of CO_2, thus already consuming around two-thirds of this budget. This means that out of the budget of 2,900 Gt, only 1,000 Gt remains to be used between now and 2100. The World Resources Institute estimates that if emissions continue unabated, the remaining budget will last only 30 more years.

The key issue, therefore, for designing emission reduction commitment is how this remaining sparse carbon budget should be allocated between countries in a manner which is both fair and achievable. This certainly should involve an assessment of historic responsibility based on how countries have contributed to cumulative emissions so far. India's contribution to cumulative global CO_2 (1850-2011) was a meagre 3 percent as against 21 percent by the US and 18 percent by the EU. The sustainability of the world economic system also needs to be analysed through the lens of social justice and equity. For developing countries, their future commitment will also be determined by what kind and level of financial, capacity-building, and other support is provided by developed countries that have contributed most to cumulative global GHG emissions so far.

There are multiple mitigation pathways that are likely to limit warming to below 2°C relative to pre-industrial levels. These pathways would require substantial emissions reduction over the next few decades and near zero emissions of CO_2 and other long-lived GHGs by the end of the century. Implementing such reductions poses substantial technological, economic, social, and institutional challenges.

13.2 Consequences of Climate Change

Changes observed in the IPCC Assessment Reports include: (a) shrinkage of glaciers, (b) thawing of permafrost, (c) lengthening of mid-to-high latitude growing seasons, (d) poleward and altitudinal shifts of plant and animal ranges, (e) decline in population of some plants and animals, (f) earlier flowering of trees and (g) changes in emergence of insects, and egg-laying in birds. Associations between changes in regional temperatures and the observed changes in physical and biological systems have been documented in many aquatic, terrestrial, and marine environments.

Changing environmental attributes are sure to affect the species spectrum and depending upon the pace of change, the profile and composition of forests is also likely to change. In arid or semi-arid areas, productivity is expected to decrease. Trends of drying up of wetlands and degradation of ecosystems have been observed.

The water cycle is totally dependent on the temperature regime. Increasing global temperature and resultant faster retreat of most glaciers is expected to affect the snow-fed perennial water regimes. Accordingly, the vegetation status of catchments, magnitude and frequency of floods, precipitation, run-off and groundwater recharge may be affected. It may substantially affect hydropower generation and increase in irrigation withdrawal, due to higher crop evaporative demand.

Changes in the frequencies of extreme heat and cold, the frequencies of floods and droughts, and the profile of local air pollution may result in changes in occurrence of infectious diseases, leading to impaired child development and various health consequences of population displacement and economic disruption.

Estimates of crop yield responses to climate change vary widely, depending upon species, cultivation practices, soil properties, and direct effects of carbon dioxide (CO_2) on plants. Even though increased CO_2 concentration can stimulate crop growth and yield that benefit may not always overcome the adverse effects of excessive heat and drought.

In countries with predominantly agrarian economies, increase in temperature and reduction in precipitation could—in the absence of adequate irrigation and related infrastructural interventions—dampen the economic growth by reducing agricultural productivity. These impacts can be moderated by efforts at adaptation but these are expected to be costly and will impose a burden on both producers and consumers.

For South Asia, warming has been predicted to be above the global mean and in Southeast Asia, equal to the global mean. Precipitation is likely to increase and extreme rainfall and other climatic events may occur more frequently. For India, extreme rains in South West monsoon and fewer rainy days along East Coast have been predicted.

For India and China, risks of dengue fever have been predicted by IPCC. Increase in flooding is associated with increased risk of drowning, diarrhoeal and respiratory diseases, and hunger and malnutrition.

Adaptive options like health-oriented management of the environment (including air and water quality, food safety, urban and housing design, and surface water management), and appropriate medical interventions are normally related to income levels. Therefore, poor income levels are more vulnerable. Human settlements are expected to be accordingly affected by changes in resource productivity or market demand for the goods and services causing structural and functional adaptations leading to migration, and resultant living conditions. Climate change would, therefore, result in increase in the absolute number of people at risk of hunger unless these outcomes can be countered through the development of cost effective technologies.

Recognizing the importance of these issues, the Prime Minister has established an Advisory Council on Climate Change including eminent experts to advice on climate change issues. The Council has been tasked with preparing a National Action Plan on Climate Change.

13.3 United Nations Framework Convention on Climate Change (UNFCCC)

Recognizing the problem and the need for international co-operation, the international community in 1992 established the UNFCCC which accepted the principle of *common but differentiated responsibility* between the industrialized countries and the developing countries.

The objective of UNFCCC is to achieve stabilization of greenhouse gas concentrations in the atmosphere at a level that would prevent dangerous anthropogenic interference with the climate system. The Convention enjoins Parties to communicate information about the implementation of the Convention, taking into account the common but differentiated responsibilities and respective capabilities and their specific regional and national development priorities, objectives and circumstances. Article 12 of the Convention relates to the communication of information pertaining to implementation in accordance with Article 4(1) of the Convention, whereby each Party is required to communicate to the Conference of the Parties. The elements of information in the communication are provided in the context of national circumstances and include the following:

1. A national inventory of anthropogenic emissions by sources and removals by sinks of all greenhouse gases not controlled by the Montreal Protocol, to the extent its capacities permit, using comparable methodologies to be promoted and agreed upon by the Conference of Parties.
2. A general description of steps taken to implement the

Convention including an assessment of impacts, vulnerability due to climate change and associated adaptation needs.

3. Any other information that the Party considers relevant to the achievement of the objective of the Convention and suitable for inclusion in its communication, including, if feasible, material relevant for calculations of global emission trends.

13.3.1 Kyoto Protocol: In 1997, Parties signatory to UNFCCC adopted the Kyoto Protocol which set legally binding targets for GHG reductions by individual industrialized countries during *first commitment period, 2008-12*, totalling 5.2 percent below their aggregate 1990 emissions. The Protocol did not involve any binding commitments by developing countries in recognition of the fact that historically it was the industrialized countries that were responsible for the overwhelming bulk of the stock of GHGs.

Kyoto Protocol made provisions for use of any of the three mechanisms including the Clean Development Mechanism (CDM) to help developed countries meet their quantified emission limitation and reduction commitments domestically and through acquisition of greenhouse gas reduction credits from activities outside their own boundaries at relatively lesser costs. India is a major participant in the projects aimed at using Clean Development Mechanism.

Kyoto Protocol took a more *top-down* but highly differentiated approach, establishing negotiated, binding emissions targets for developed countries, and no new commitments for developing countries.

175 countries including India ratified the Protocol. The US and some other countries did not ratify the Protocol. As it happens, most of those that did ratify the protocol have failed to live up to the commitments they had undertaken.

Under the provisions of the Kyoto Protocol, India as a non-annex I party, is not obliged to reduce emission of GHG. Under the Asia-Pacific Partnership on Clean Development and Climate, India has also been working with the US, Australia, China, Japan and Republic of Korea on possible development and promotion of clean technologies for dealing with climate change.

Kyoto Protocol came to an end in 2012.

13.3.2 Copenhagen Accord and Cancún Agreements: With the Copenhagen Accord (2009) and Cancún Agreements (2010), parties established a parallel *bottom-up* framework, with countries undertaking national pledges for 2020 that represented political rather than legal commitments. This approach attracted much wider participation, including, for the first time, specific mitigation pledges by developing countries. However, countries' pledges fell far short of the reductions needed to meet the goal set in Copenhagen and Cancún of keeping average warming below 2 degrees Celsius above pre-industrial levels.

13.3.3 Paris Agreement, 2015: The negotiations toward a Paris agreement were launched with the Durban Platform for Enhanced Action adopted at Seventeenth Conference of Parties (COP 17) in 2011. The Durban Platform called for *a protocol, another legal instrument or an agreed outcome with legal force under the Convention applicable to all Parties*, to apply from 2020, but provided no further substantive guidance.

COP 19 in Warsaw called on parties to submit *intended nationally determined contributions* (INDCs) well before the Paris conference, signalling an important bottom-up feature of the emerging agreement. Heading into Paris, more than 180 countries producing more than 90 percent of global emissions had submitted INDCs, a much broader response than many had anticipated.

The Paris Agreement marks the latest step in the evolution of the UN climate change regime, which originated in 1992 with the adoption of the Framework Convention. The UNFCCC established a long-term objective, general principles, common and differentiated commitments, and a basic governance structure, including an annual Conference of Parties (COP).

The U.N. Climate Change Conference in Paris (November 30 to December 12, 2015) presented a critical opportunity for parties to the U.N. Framework Convention on Climate Change

(UNFCCC) to strengthen the global response to climate change. The negotiating mandate for the Paris talks called for a post-2020 climate agreement under the UNFCCC *with legal force* and *applicable to all Parties*. In fulfilling this mandate, the Paris conference was asked to produce a package: a core legal agreement and related instruments and decisions.

Parties to the UNFCCC reached a landmark agreement on December 12, 2015 in Paris, charting a fundamentally new course in the two-decade-old global climate effort.

Culminating a four-year negotiating round, the new treaty ended the strict differentiation between developed and developing countries that characterized earlier efforts, replacing it with a common framework that commits all countries to put forward their best efforts and to strengthen them in the years ahead. This included, for the first time, requirements that all parties report regularly on their emissions and implementation efforts, and undergo international review.

A. Highlights of Paris Agreement: The agreement and a companion decision by parties were the key outcomes of the conference, known as the 21st session of the UNFCCC Conference of the Parties (or COP 21). The Paris Agreement:

1. Reaffirmed the goal of limiting global temperature increase well below 2 degrees Celsius, while urging efforts to limit the increase to 1.5 degrees.
2. Established binding commitments by all parties to make *nationally determined contributions* (NDCs), and to pursue domestic measures aimed at achieving them.
3. Committed all countries to report regularly on their emissions and *progress made in implementing and achieving* their NDCs, and to undergo international review.
4. Committed all countries to submit new NDCs every five years, with the clear expectation that they will *represent a progression* beyond previous ones.
5. Reaffirmed the binding obligations of developed countries under the UNFCCC to support the efforts of developing

countries, while for the first time encouraging voluntary contributions by developing countries too.

6. Extended the current goal of mobilizing US$ 100 billion a year in support by 2020 through 2025, with a new, higher goal to be set for the period after 2025.
7. Extended a mechanism to address *loss and damage* resulting from climate change, which explicitly will not *involve or provide a basis for any liability or compensation.*
8. Required parties engaging in international emissions trading to avoid *double counting.*
9. Called for a new mechanism, similar to the Clean Development Mechanism under the Kyoto Protocol, enabling emission reductions in one country to be counted toward another country's NDC.

The strong momentum toward an agreement that built over the preceding months was dramatically underscored on the opening day of the summit by the presence of 150 presidents and prime ministers, the largest ever single-day gathering of heads of state. Impetus came also from a vast array of *non-state actors*, including governors, mayors and CEOs, and the launch in Paris of major initiatives like the Breakthrough Energy Coalition announced by Bill Gates and other billionaires.

Negotiations on many issues were hard-fought and, in typical COP fashion, progress through most of the conference was painstakingly slow. But thanks to deft diplomacy by the French presidency, the summit was remarkably free of the kind of procedural showdowns that marred previous COPs.

Many operational details of the new framework were left to be decided by future COPs. The agreement will take effect only once enough countries have formally ratified it.

B. Paris Agreement: Salient Features: In broad structure, the Paris Agreement reflects a *hybrid* approach blending bottom-up flexibility, to achieve broad participation, with top-down rules, to promote accountability and ambition.

(a) Legal Character: The Paris Agreement is a treaty under international law, but only certain provisions are legally binding.

The issue of which provisions to make binding (expressed as *shall*, as opposed to *should*) was a central concern for many countries, in particular the United States, which wanted an agreement the president could accept without seeking congressional approval. Meeting that test precluded binding emission targets and new binding financial commitments.

A final step in Paris was negotiating a *technical correction* substituting *should* for *shall* in a provision calling on developed countries to undertake absolute economy-wide emissions targets.

(b) Differentiation: A cross-cutting issue was how to reflect the UNFCCC's principle of *common but differentiated responsibilities and respective capabilities*. On the whole, the Paris Agreement represented a fundamental shift away from the categorical binary approach of the Kyoto Protocol toward more nuanced forms of differentiation, reflected differently in different provisions.

The agreement includes references to developed and developing countries, stating in several places that the former should take the lead. But it notably makes no mention of the Annex I (developed) and non-Annex I (developing) categories contained in the UNFCCC.

Many provisions establish common commitments while allowing flexibility to accommodate different national capacities and circumstances—either through self-differentiation, as implicit in the concept of *nationally determined* contributions, or through more detailed operational rules still to be developed.

(c) Long-Term Goal: The agreement reaffirms the goal of keeping average warming below 2 degrees Celsius, while also urging parties to *pursue efforts* to limit it to 1.5 degrees, a top priority for developing countries highly vulnerable to climate impacts.

(d) Mitigation: The Paris Agreement articulates two long-term emission goals: first, a peaking of emissions as soon as possible (with a recognition that it will take longer for developing countries); then, a goal of net greenhouse gas neutrality (expressed as *a balance between anthropogenic emissions by sources and removals by sinks*) in the second half of this century. The latter was an alternative to terms like *decarbonization* and *climate neutrality* pushed by some parties.

With respect to countries' individual mitigation efforts, the agreement prescribes a set of binding procedural commitments: to *prepare, communicate and maintain* an NDC; to provide information necessary for clarity and transparency; and to communicate a new NDC every five years. It also sets the expectation that each successive NDC will *represent a progression* beyond the previous one and reflect a party's *highest possible ambition.*

The agreement commits parties to *pursue domestic measures with the aim of achieving the objectives* of its NDC, but does not make the implementation or achievement of NDCs a binding obligation. It also encourages, but does not require, countries to develop and communicate long-term low emission development strategies.

The core mitigation commitments are common to all parties, but there is some differentiation in the expectations set: developed countries *should* undertake absolute economy-wide reduction targets, while developing countries *are encouraged* to move toward economy-wide targets over time. In addition, developing countries are to receive support to implement their commitments.

NDCs will be recorded in a public registry maintained by the UNFCCC secretariat, rather than in an annex to the agreement, as some countries had proposed.

(e) Carbon Markets: While avoiding any direct reference to the use of market-based approaches—a concession to a handful of countries that oppose them—the agreement recognizes that parties may use *internationally transferred* *mitigation outcomes* to implement their NDCs.

It requires that parties engaging in such transfers ensure the *avoidance of double counting*, consistent with accounting guidelines for NDCs to be developed. The agreement also establishes a new mechanism to succeed the Kyoto Protocol's Clean Development Mechanism, which generates tradable emission offsets. Rules for the new mechanism are to be adopted at the first meeting of parties after the agreement takes force.

(f) Stocktake/Successive NDCs: To promote rising ambition, the agreement establishes two linked processes, each on a five-year cycle.

The first process is a *global stocktake* to assess collective progress toward meeting the agreement's long-term goals. The first stock take will take place in 2023. The second process is the submission by parties of new NDCs, *informed by the outcomes of the global stocktake*.

Because these processes technically begin only once the agreement takes force, the accompanying decision includes provisions to effectively jumpstart them in the interim. It establishes a *facilitative dialogue* in 2018 to take stock of collective progress. And, by 2020, countries like the United States whose initial NDCs run through 2025 are *urged* to communicate *new* NDCs, while those whose initial NDCs run through 2030 are *requested* to *communicate or update* theirs.

(g) Transparency: The Paris Agreement rests heavily on transparency as a means of holding countries accountable. In another move beyond bifurcation, it establishes a new transparency system with common binding commitments for all parties and *built-in flexibility* to accommodate varying national capacities.

All countries are required to submit emissions inventories and the *information necessary to track progress made in implementing and achieving* their NDCs. The COP decision says that, with the exception of least developed and small island countries, these reports are to be submitted at least every two years. In addition, developed countries *shall* report on support provided; developing countries *should* report on support received; and all *should* report on their adaptation efforts.

Information reported by countries on mitigation and support will undergo *expert technical review*, and each party must participate in *a facilitative, multilateral consideration of progress* in implementing and achieving its NDC (a form of peer review).

Developing countries are promised capacity-building support to help them meet the new transparency requirements. The COP decision says they will be given flexibility in the scope, frequency and detail of their reporting, and in the scope of review. Details of the new transparency system are to be negotiated by 2018 and formally adopted once the agreement enters into force.

(h) Implementation/Compliance: The agreement establishes a new mechanism to *facilitate implementation* and *promote compliance*. The mechanism—a committee of experts—is to be *facilitative* in nature and operate in a *non-adversarial and non-punitive* manner. It will report annually to the COP. Details are to be decided at the first meeting of parties after the agreement takes force.

(i) Finance: As at past COPs, finance was a contentious issue in Paris, with poorer developing countries seeking stronger assurances that support will be scaled up, and developed countries pushing for wealthier developing countries to contribute as well.

Both succeeded to some degree. The agreement commits developed countries to provide finance for mitigation and adaptation in developing countries (*in continuation of their existing obligations under the Convention*, a stipulation sought by the United States so the agreement would not create new binding financial commitments requiring congressional approval). *Other* parties are *encouraged* to provide such support *voluntarily*.

Other major issues included whether to set a new finance mobilization goal beyond the US$ 100 billion a year in public and private resources already promised by developed countries, and whether to establish a process to revisit the question every five years. The COP decision extends the US$ 100 billion-a-year goal through 2025, and beyond that, says only that by 2025 the COP will set a *new collective quantified goal from a floor of* US$ 100 billion a year.

In addition to reporting on finance already provided and received, developed countries commit to submit every two years, *indicative quantitative and qualitative information* on future support, including, *as available*, projected levels of public finance; and other countries are encouraged to do so voluntarily. Finance will also be considered in the global stocktake.

(j) Adaptation: A major priority for many developing countries was strengthening adaptation efforts under the UNFCCC. The agreement does that by:

1. Establishing a global goal of *enhancing adaptive capacity, strengthening resilience and reducing vulnerability to climate change.*
2. Requiring all parties, *as appropriate*, to plan and implement adaptation efforts.
3. Encouraging all parties to report on their adaptation efforts and/or needs.
4. Committing enhanced adaptation support for developing countries.
5. Including a review of adaptation progress, and of the adequacy and effectiveness of adaptation support, in the global stocktake to be undertaken every five years.

(k) Loss and Damage: In a victory for small island countries and other countries highly vulnerable to climate impacts, the agreement includes a free-standing provision extending the Warsaw International Mechanism for Loss and Damage.

The mechanism, established as an interim body at COP 19, is charged with developing approaches to help vulnerable countries cope with unavoidable impacts, including extreme weather events and slow-onset events such as sea-level rise. Potential approaches include early warning systems and risk insurance.

At the insistence of developed countries, led by the United States, the accompanying COP decision specifies that the loss and damage provision *does not involve or provide a basis for any liability or compensation.*

(l) Next Steps: The Paris Agreement will be open for signature on April 22, 2016. In order to become a party to the agreement, a country must then express it consent to be bound through a formal process of ratification, acceptance, approval or accession (different terms for essentially the same thing). Each country has its own domestic procedures for deciding whether to join an international agreement.

The agreement establishes a *double trigger* for entry-into-force: it requires approval by at least 55 countries accounting for at least 55 percent of global greenhouse gas emissions. If states ratify quickly, these conditions could be satisfied pre-2020, allowing the COP to begin meeting as the *meeting of the Parties* to the Paris Agreement, to be known by the acronym CMA.

In the meantime, pending the agreement's entry into force, a new Ad Hoc Working Group on the Paris Agreement was formed to consider issues requiring further rules or guidance. On October 5, 2016, the threshold for entry into force of the Paris Agreement was achieved with 136 out of the 197 parties to the Convention, ratifying the Agreement. The Paris Agreement entered into force on November 4, 2016. The first session of the Conference of the Parties serving as the Meeting of the Parties to the Paris Agreement (CMA 1) took place in Marrakech, Morocco from November 15-18, 2016.

To sum up, the serious consequences of climate change lead naturally to the question of what should be the response. Two types of responses need to be considered. The first relates to adaptation, i.e. measures that have to be taken given the very high likelihood that climate change will occur and will have adverse effects. The second relates to mitigation, i.e.

steps to be taken that might reduce the extent of climate change. The two are clearly interconnected. The more effective the mitigation strategy, the less society has to worry about adaptation. Likewise, if mitigation is not likely to be effective, or cannot be organised effectively, then adaptation acquires special urgency.

Endnote

1. Bali Action Plan on Technological Options, agreed in December 2007, launched a comprehensive process to enable the full, effective and sustained implementation of the United Nations Framework Convention on Climate Change (UNFCCC, 2007) through long-term cooperative action, now, up to and beyond 2012, in order to reach an agreed outcome and adopt a decision in Copenhagen in December 2009. The Bali Action Plan attaches equal weight to mitigation and adaptation, and identifies technology and finance as the key mechanisms to enable developing countries to respond to climate change. Recent years have seen a surge in research and policy analysis on ways in which technology and finance can support mitigation. Similar studies for adaptation are much more recent, and their results therefore less mature.

   The traditional view of adaptation tends to assume that a national government is responsible for implementing technological adaptation measures (e.g. new seed varieties, dams, early-warning systems and irrigation schemes) based on specific knowledge of future climate conditions.

   Even though climate science has made great advances over the past years, it often remains difficult to project future impacts of climate change in sufficient detail to justify investment in technological adaptation measures, in particular on a local scale. An important uncertainty relates to the effect of a changing climate on the frequency, magnitude and spatial occurrence of extreme weather events, such as floods, cyclones and droughts. Planning specific measures based on projections of future climate conditions therefore presents a great challenge to developing countries.

14

International Efforts and Co-operation

Global interfaces are gaining increasing importance in the field of environment. Environment is characterised by interconnectedness that transcends national/international boundaries and hence international cooperation and national efforts are seminally important to achieve the objectives of equitable access to clean air and water, adaptation and mitigation of climate change, conservation of biodiversity, sustainable forest management, safety in the management of chemicals, wastes and other hazardous substances.

14.1 International Union for Conservation of Nature (IUCN)

IUCN is a unique global organization which started working in 1948. It is one of the handfuls of international organizations where governments and non-governmental bodies work together as parties. By virtue of being a member of IUCN, a country has access to the largest network of specialists in the field of conservation. IUCN is having an observer status at the United Nations and advises governments on matters related to conservation, integrity and diversity of nature and also ensures that any use of natural resources is equitable and ecologically sustainable.

India has a long relationship with IUCN. The Government of India was the first country in South Asia to join IUCN as a state member in 1969. It was also the first country in the region to host the General Assembly of IUCN in 1969.

14.2 United Nations Environment Programme (UNEP)

UNEP, established in 1972 after the Rio Earth Summit, is the principal entity within the UN System to assist the developing countries in building scientific and technical capacity, fostering partnership and knowledge development to promote environment for sustainable development. Based in Nairobi (Kenya), UNEP activities range from assessment of environmental trends—especially early warning systems to deal with environmental disasters and emergencies—to promotion of environmental science and information.

One of the main responsibilities of UNEP is to keep under review the world environmental situation and ensure that emerging environmental problems of wide international significance are prioritized and receive appropriate and adequate consideration by the governments.

14.3 Environment and Millennium Development Goals

In 2000, the 191 members of the United Nations, including India, committed to achieving 8 Millennium Development Goals by 2015. The 7th of these 8 Goals pertains to environmental sustainability:

1. **Eradicate Extreme Poverty and Hunger:**
   - Reduce by half the proportion of people living on less than a dollar a day.
   - Reduce by half the proportion of people who suffer from hunger.
2. **Achieve Universal Primary Education:**
   - Ensure that all boys and girls complete a full course of primary schooling.
3. **Promote Gender Equality and Empower Women:**
   - Eliminate gender disparity in primary and secondary education preferably by 2005, and at all levels by 2015.
4. **Reduce Child Mortality:**
   - Reduce by two thirds the mortality rate among children under five.
5. **Improve Maternal Health:**
   - Reduce by three quarters the maternal mortality ratio.
6. **Combat HIV/AIDS, Malaria and Other Diseases:**
   - Halt and begin to reverse the spread of HIV/AIDS. Halt and begin to reverse the incidence of malaria and other

major diseases.

7. **Ensure Environmental Sustainability:**

- Integrate the principles of sustainable development into country policies and programmes; reverse loss of environmental resources.
- Reduce by half the proportion of people without sustainable access to safe drinking water.
- Achieve significant improvement in lives of at least 100 million slum dwellers, by 2020.

8. **Develop a Global Partnership for Development:**

- Develop further an open trading and financial system that is rule-based, predictable and non-discriminatory, and includes a commitment to good governance, development and poverty reduction—nationally and internationally.
- Address the least developed countries' special needs. This includes tariff- and quota-free access for their exports, enhanced debt relief for heavily indebted poor countries, cancellation of official bilateral debt, and more generous official development assistance for countries committed to poverty reduction.
- Address the special needs of landlocked and small-island developing States.
- Deal comprehensively with debt problems of developing countries through national and international measures to make debt sustainable in the long-term.
- In cooperation with the developing countries, develop decent and productive work for youth.
- In cooperation with pharmaceutical companies, provide access to affordable essential drugs in developing countries.
- In cooperation with the private sector, make available the benefits of new technologies, especially information and communications technologies.

14.4 Sustainable Development Goals (SDGs)

On January 1, 2016, the 17 Sustainable Development Goals

(SDGs) of the 2030 Agenda for Sustainable Development, adopted by world leaders in September 2015 at an historic UN Summit, officially came into force.

SDGs are the blueprint to achieve a better and more sustainable future for all. They address the global challenges, including those related to poverty, inequality, climate, environmental degradation, prosperity, and peace and justice. The Goals interconnect and in order to leave no one behind, it ís important to achieve each Goal and target by 2030.

These new Goals that universally apply to all, countries will mobilize efforts to end all forms of poverty, fight inequalities and tackle climate change, while ensuring that no one is left behind.

SDGs build on the success of the Millennium Development Goals (MDGs) and aim to go further to end all forms of poverty. The new Goals are unique in that they call for action by all countries, poor, rich and middle-income to promote prosperity while protecting the planet. They recognize that ending poverty must go hand-in-hand with strategies that build economic growth and addresses a range of social needs including education, health, social protection, and job opportunities, while tackling climate change and environmental protection.

The seventeen goals are as under:

Goal 1: End poverty in all its forms.

Goal 2: Zero hunger.

Goal 3: Health.

Goal 4: Education.

Goal 5: Gender equality and women's empowerment.

Goal 6: Water and sanitation.

Goal 7: Energy.

Goal 8: Economic growth.

Goal 9: Infrastructure, industrialization.

Goal 10: Inequality.

Goal 11: Cities.

Goal 12: Sustainable consumption and production.

Goal 13: Climate change.

Goal 14: Oceans.
Goal 15: Biodiversity, forests, desertification.
Goal 16: Peace, justice and strong institutions.
Goal 17: Partnerships.

14.5 Sustainable Development Goals Report, 2018

According to this Report, a fast-changing climate, conflict, inequality, persistent pockets of poverty and hunger and rapid urbanization are challenging countries' efforts to achieve SDGs.

The Report found that conflict and climate change were major contributing factors leading to growing numbers of people facing hunger and forced displacement, as well as curtailing progress towards universal access to basic water and sanitation services.

For the first time in more than a decade, there are now approximately 38 million more hungry people in the world, rising from 777 million in 2015 to 815 million in 2016. According to the report, conflict is now one of the main drivers of food insecurity in 18 countries. In 2017, the world experienced the costliest North Atlantic hurricane season on record, driving the global economic losses attributed to the disasters to over US$ 300 billion.

At the same time, the Report found that more people are leading better lives than they were just a decade ago. The proportion of the world's workers living with their families on less than 1.90 per person a day declined significantly over the past two decades, falling from 26.9 percent in 2000 to 9.2 percent in 2017.

The under-five mortality rate dropped by almost 50 per cent and in the least developed countries, the proportion of population with access to electricity has more than doubled between 2000 and 2016. However, in 2015, 2.3 billion people still lacked even a basic level of sanitation service and 892 million people continued to practice open defecation. In 2016, there were 216 million cases of malaria compared to 210 million cases in 2013 and close to 4 billion people were left without social protection in 2016.

SDG Report presents an overview of progress toward achieving the Goals, which were unanimously adopted by countries in 2015. As the global community moves forward to achieve the SDGs and address existing challenges, reliable, timely, accessible and disaggregated data is critically needed. This requires technology and innovation, increased resources and political commitment to build strong data and statistical systems in all countries.

14.6 Economic Instruments for Promoting Sustainable Development

The role of economic instruments in financing and promoting sustainable development is well recognised. The following economic instruments can help achieve sustainable development through their influence on behavioural patterns leading to sustainable consumption and production in the economy:

14.6.1 Environmental Taxes: An environment or green tax is imposed on a product that damages the environment, in an attempt to reduce its production or consumption. Well-designed environmental taxes and other economic instruments can play an important role in ensuring that prices reflect environmental costs, in line with the *polluter pays principle*. Environmental taxes can be simple and efficient financial instruments for improving the productivity of natural resources. Environmental taxes on water and fossil fuels need not be part of the general revenues of the Government. Rather they should be directly ploughed back into environmentally sustainable action on these fronts. Coal Cess is a good example of environment tax imposed by Government of India in recent times, whose proceeds are channelled to the National Clean Energy Fund. Some benefits of environment taxation are enumerated below:

1. They provide incentives for measures that protect the

environment, and deter actions that lead to environmental damage.

2. Economic instruments such as taxes can enable environmental goals to be achieved at the lowest cost, and in the most efficient way.
3. By internalizing environmental costs into prices, they help signal the structural economic changes needed to move to a more sustainable economy.
4. They can encourage innovation and development of new technology.
5. The revenue raised by environmental taxes can be used to reduce the level of other taxes. This could help reduce distortions, while raising the efficiency with which resources are used in the economy.

14.6.2 Subsidies: There has been a growing recognition of fiscal and environmental implications of the subsidy policies in energy, water and agriculture sectors. Most of these subsidies pose a threat to the environment. For example, in India, the subsidy on diesel has distorted the use of energy in transport and industrial sectors, and worsened the problem of hazardous air pollution. Similarly, excessive use of nitrogenous fertilizers and over-drawing of water, backed by subsidies at both Centre and State levels, is playing havoc with the sustainability of soil and water ecosystem.

14.6.3 Non-monetary Incentives: Non-monetary incentives are policy instruments that typically do not have a monetary value, but definitely have a financial impact that promotes sustainability. These incentives can be used as a bargaining tool by the Government to encourage conservation of resources in an economy. Activities such as those encouraging judicious use of water, planting trees, car pooling and avoiding use of plastic bags can be rewarded so that it encourages the practice, and acts as an example for others. Through the initiation of innovative policies and awards, the Government can provide recognition, which will encourage sustainable development amongst the citizens and the firms.

14.6.4 Eco-Industrial Hubs: An eco-industrial park (EIP) or estate is a community of manufacturing and service businesses located together on a common property. Member businesses seek enhanced environmental, economic and social performance through collaboration in managing environmental and resource issues. By working together, the community of businesses seeks a collective benefit that is greater than the sum of individual benefits each company would realise by only optimizing its individual performance.

The goal of an EIP is to improve the economic performance of the participating companies while minimizing their environmental impacts. Components of this approach include green design of the park infrastructure (new or retrofitted); cleaner production; prevention of pollution; energy efficiency and inter-company partnering. An EIP also seeks benefits for neighbouring communities to assure the net impact of its development is positive.

To sum up, sustainable development is a pattern of social and structured economic transformations (i.e. development) which optimizes the economic and social benefits available at present, without jeopardizing the likely potential for similar benefits in the future. The primary goal of sustainable development is to achieve a reasonable and equitable distribution level of economic well being that can be perpetuated continually for the future human generations.

Sustainability is about meeting the needs of the present without compromising the ability of future generations to meet their needs. It is about preserving the environment and biodiversity for future generations, and about being cautious with our natural resources and climate. But sustainability is also about guaranteeing human rights and a life in dignity, free from want and poverty for all people living today.

Developing countries have options other than to *grow dirty and clean up later*. Much that is useful can be done now. Clean air and water and solid waste management are basic needs, and many environmental policies enhance productivity and poverty alleviation. So while poor countries should focus on meeting basic needs and expanding opportunities for growth, they need not do so at the expense of unsustainable environmental degradation. Further, environmental performance does not automatically improve with income, so policy action is needed anyway. Finally, it may be impossible or prohibitively expensive to *clean up later*, either because of the irreversibility of environmental damages like the loss of biodiversity, or because "lock-in" will make subsequent shifts to more environmentally benign structures and processes extremely costly.

Bibliography

Alexander, J.W. (1963), "Economic Geography", Prentice-Hall, New Jersey.

Bagchi, P., Sen, S. and Smith, H.L. (2006), "Economic Geography: Past, Present and Future", Taylor and Francis.

Briceno-Garmendia, C., Estache, A. and Shafik, N. (2004), "Infrastructure Services in Developing Countries: Access, Quality, Costs and Policy Reform", World Bank Policy Research, Working Paper No. 3468.

Chandna, R.C. (2010), "Population Geography", Kalyani Publishers.

Dandekar, V.M. (1996), "Population, Poverty and Employment", Sage Publications India Pvt. Ltd., New Delhi.

ESCAP (1994), "Infrastructure Development as Key to Economic Growth and Regional Economic Cooperation", United Nations.

ESCAP (1997), "Mobilising Private Sector Resources for Infrastructure", United Nations.

Goudie, A. (2001), "The Nature of the Environment", Blackwell, Oxford.

Hammer, Marks Jr. and Hammer Jr., Mark J. (2002), "Water and Waste Technology", Prentice Hall of India Pvt. Ltd, New Delhi.

Hazell, P.B. and Haggblade, S. (1991), "Rural-Urban Growth Linkages in India", *Indian Journal of Agricultural Economics,* Volume 46.

Jerry, A. Nathanson (2002), "Basic Environmental Technology", fourth edition, Prentice Hall of India Pvt. Ltd., New Delhi.

Karpagam, M. (1999), "Environment Economics", Sterling Publications, Chennai

Mall, R.K., Kumar, R. and Bhatla, R. (2010), "Climate Change and Disasters in India", *Journal of South Asia Disaster Studies,* SAARC Disaster Management Centre, New Delhi.

Mody, A. (1997), "Infrastructure Strategies in East Asia", World Bank Economic Development Institute, Learning Resources Series.

Mody, A. (ed.) (1996), "Infrastructure Delivery and the Public Good", World Bank, Washington D.C.

Naidu, G. (1998), "Mobilising Resources for Infrastructure: The Experience in Mobilising Private Sector Resources for

Infrastructure", ESCAP, United Nations.

Rajaraman, Indira (2005), "Financing Rural Infrastructure in Developing Countries", *Applied Econometrics and International Development,* Volume 5.

United Nations (2003), "Millennium Development Goals and the United Nations Role".

——"World Economic and Social Survey" (various years).

World Bank (1994), "Infrastructure for Development", World Development Report.

——"World Development Report" (various years).

——"Gender and Poverty in India: A World Bank Country Study", 1991.

Yamazawa, Ippei (2000), "Developing Economies in the Twenty-First Century: The Challenge of Globalisation", Institute of Developing Economies, Japan.

Index

Index